NEURODIVERSE
IS THE NEW
NORMAL
EMBRACE YOUR UNIQUE MIND

Joe Bradley

Copyright © 2025 by Joe Bradley All rights reserved.

No portion of this book may be reproduced in any form without written permission from the publisher or author, except as permitted by U.S. copyright law.

This publication is designed to share personal insights and opinions regarding neurodiversity. It is sold with the understanding that neither the author nor the publisher is engaged in providing medical, psychological, legal, or any other professional services. The content in this book is not intended to diagnose, treat, or cure any medical condition, nor should it be used as a substitute for professional medical or psychological advice. While the author has made every effort to provide accurate information based on personal experience and research, neither the author nor the publisher makes any representations or warranties regarding the accuracy or completeness of the information presented.

This book reflects the author's opinions and is not intended to represent established medical or scientific facts. The strategies and perspectives shared may not be suitable for every individual, and readers are encouraged to consult with qualified professionals for advice tailored to their specific circumstances. Neither the author nor the publisher shall be liable for any damages, personal or commercial, that may arise from the application of the information in this book.

Book Cover by Joe Bradley

1st edition 2025

Contents

DEDICATION	1
SYNOPSIS	3
PREFACE	5
EMBRACING NEURODIVERGENCE STARTS WITH UNDERSTANDING	35
EMBRACING YOUR STRENGTHS	87
IT'S TIME TO RISE.	125
NAVIGATING THE NEUROTYPICAL WORLD	150
MENTAL HEALTH; IT MATTERS.	240
EXPLORING THE SPECTRUM OF NEURODIVERSITY	309
SELF EMPOWERMENT	378
YOU ARE CAPABLE OF ANYTHING	395
About The Author	416

DEDICATION

This book is for my family. To my wife, Heather—without you, none of this would even be possible. You're my anchor, my constant, and life before you doesn't even compare to what we've built together. You push me to be better every single day.

To my son, CJ—your autism has changed our lives in ways I couldn't have imagined, and it's made us stronger. I love you more than words can say, and I want you to know that your future is wide open. It's yours to shape however you want.

To my daughter, Liv—you're a force. Your drive, your heart, and your relentless pursuit of everything you set your mind to inspires me daily. You remind me to just keep pushing forward, no matter what.

SYNOPSIS

I could have filled this book with the struggles, complaints, and challenges that come with being autistic, having ADHD, and raising a child with autism. **But I won't**. This isn't about what's wrong with the world or the endless battles that come with being neurodivergent. **This book is about reframing those struggles**—because while not everyone has the ability to embrace the opportunity within their challenges, I do. So I must.

Neurodiverse Is The New Normal is a deeply personal and straightforward guide to embracing your differences and learning to thrive, not despite them, but because of them. It's for anyone who has ever felt stuck, misunderstood, or out of place in a world designed for neurotypicals. Through my own experiences, collected insights, and a lifetime of trial and error, I've discovered ways to adapt, grow, and redefine what success looks like for people like us.

But let's be clear: I'm not a doctor, therapist, or researcher. I don't have degrees or credentials, and the information in this book isn't meant to replace professional advice. Everything here is based on my own life, my observations, and my collected research, which might not be perfect—or even entirely accurate. This is my story, my findings, and my perspective. You're encouraged to dig deeper, ask questions, and do your own research to decide what works best for you.

If you're ready to stop focusing on what's wrong and start seeing what's possible, this book is for you. It's not about waiting for society to change; it's about making the most of who you are right now and building a life that works for you. Because being neurodiverse isn't just normal—it's powerful.

PREFACE

One of the moments that changed my life—and my earliest memory of realizing I was different—happened in 8th grade. Growing up as an only child to a single mother in the 80s, I often craved attention, anything to prove that I mattered. I remember feeling special when I was asked to help in the special needs classroom. I thought, "Wow, they know I love helping teachers." This realization came after the teacher kicked me out of class for being disruptive during a group exercise. I don't remember the exact reason, but it wasn't unusual for me to end up in the principal's office. The staff recognized me by name, and I made being sent there feel like a normal routine, so it never seemed like a punishment. In hindsight, I knew that the principal's waiting room was more welcoming and comfortable than the classroom.

During one of my routine visits, a nurse approached me and asked if I wanted to leave science class early each day to help her in the special needs room. She described the kids there as full of energy and often misunderstood—like me! I hated science class, especially because of the teacher's pet, Becky. I had a crush on her, but she clearly hated how I always stole the spotlight with my antics.

When I first started leaving science class to help in the special needs room, I had no idea how different these kids were. I still remember the flood of sensations that hit me as soon as I walked in—the distinct smell, the deep quiet, and the eerie stillness of the room. But what struck me most was the overwhelming sadness as I realized how much these kids needed help. Within the first hour, I learned that some of them needed their diapers changed, and most were confined to wheelchairs, unable to even wipe the spit from their own mouths.

I had no idea how I was going to help; I could barely take care of myself. For a moment, I thought I'd be better off in science class after all. The sadness of the situation hit me hard, and I must have shown it on my face because the nurse who invited me rushed over, telling me to sit down and breathe. I told her I didn't know how to help, that I should probably go back to class. But in the calmest voice—one that still resonates with me today—she explained that the only thing I needed to do was be myself and be a friend.

She then sat me next to Stephanie, a girl in a wheelchair with cerebral palsy. The nurse told me that Stephanie was incredibly smart, but unable to speak or move much. She could only express her feelings through sounds and facial expressions. When I realized that there was a real person, with thoughts and emotions just like me, trapped in a body that wouldn't let her get the words out, I was completely overwhelmed. I started to cry, and I still remember that feeling vividly.

Over the next few months, Stephanie became a close friend as I sat with her and read to her every day. I became the helper I'd promised to be, but it went deeper than just helping the nurse—it helped me understand something about myself. In many ways, I was just like Stephanie. I couldn't express my thoughts, feelings, or emotions the way I wanted to, and it often led to frustration. Trying to be funny in stressful situations became my outlet, which, of course, only got me into more trouble.

What I didn't realize back then was that I needed a friend. At the time, I didn't have any. Sure, I'd had friends before, but since my mom moved around so much, I was always the new kid, forced to start over again and again—13 different schools from kindergarten through 12th grade. It wasn't until we landed at this school that we stayed in one place long enough for me to settle in. But by then, I had already become "the weird kid."

In the special needs class, there were no other kids like me. None of them could go to the bathroom on their own, none could communicate without help, and most couldn't handle basic functions the way I could. They needed support, real support. And in that moment, I realized something I hadn't before—I needed help too. I needed someone who understood how lonely I was. I didn't realize it until I got pulled from science class. I was actually excited to see Stephanie. More importantly, I considered her a friend.

I'll never forget the way her whole face lit up when I walked into the room. That smile—it was like she was waiting for me. It was clear to me then that she saw me as her friend, too. One day, the nurse—Nancy—told me Stephanie had been having a rough time all day. She wouldn't stop making loud sounds during reading time; she refused to eat, and her mood had been sour since morning. I was nervous about sitting next to her, afraid that I'd somehow make things worse. But the moment she saw me, she let out a sigh of relief, and her smile—God, her smile lit up my entire day. When I waved to her, she laughed, and I'm sure my smile was as big as hers.

We needed each other. She was my friend. I still wonder where she is today, what her life has been like. She helped me through one of the hardest days of my early life, a day I'll never forget. I'll tell you about that in a moment—but first, let's go back to science class.

Matt was the kind of kid who was always smiling, always easygoing. It made it easy to think we were friends. In class, he'd help me with assignments and even chat with me during group work. It felt like I belonged, at least for a while. But looking back, I can see that our connection didn't really go beyond those moments. We didn't hang out after school or talk outside of class. He was nice—kind, even—but that wasn't the same as being a friend.

I didn't fully realize the difference until I started helping in the special needs room. Slowly, the kids I thought were friends stopped talking to me as much. Matt didn't ignore me, but there was definitely a shift. We didn't sit together as often, and the easy conversations became more distant. It wasn't anything dramatic, just a quiet realization that being friendly wasn't the same as being a real friend.

One day, after coming back from my time in the special needs room, Matt casually mentioned that the science project was due tomorrow. My heart stopped. *What science project?!* I had no memory of ever being told about a project, let alone that we'd had six months to work on it. Apparently, the whole thing was discussed during the part of class I left every day. I could feel panic rising in my chest.

I tried explaining this to the teacher, telling him I didn't even know there was a project, and I needed an extension. I remember his response so clearly: "You've been given enough of a handicap, and I won't enable you anymore." I was stunned. *What handicap?* At the time, I didn't know golf terminology, so I thought he was just calling me names. I walked back to my desk, my mind spinning, trying to figure out why this teacher hated me so much.

Matt told me he was making a volcano—something he'd seen on TV. Becky, of course, was doing a full model of the solar system, and the entire class had supplies and materials scattered around their desks, working on their projects. I just sat there with my backpack and a few crumpled papers, completely unprepared. I leaned over to Matt and told him it wasn't a big deal—I'd just show up and take the F like I usually did with homework. But then Matt dropped a bombshell.

"This isn't just some regular homework," he said. "It's your final. If you fail this, you could fail the entire class and get held back."

I don't know if that was actually true, but it hit me hard. Suddenly, the reality of failing science—and maybe the whole grade—kicked me into gear.

To this day, I've realized that when the pressure hits, I tend to perform not just well, but at my absolute best. It's like my brain switches into overdrive. What I didn't understand back then is that this isn't just a bad habit—it's part of how my mind works. I now know that my issue is likely executive dysfunction. It explains my chronic procrastination. But here's the thing: I don't see it as just a flaw. That same tendency to put things off has also been the birthplace of some of my best creative work.

At the last minute, when most people are too stressed to think clearly, something kicks in for me. It's like the chaos forces my brain to focus in ways it normally can't. I've created my best art, my best ideas, and some of my most thoughtful solutions when the clock is ticking down. What took me years to figure out, though, is that I'm not really "putting off" the work until the last minute—I'm letting my brain prepare. I'm giving it space to mull things over, think through problems, and get ready for that final sprint. When the time comes, everything clicks into place, and I can push out what feels like magic.

I still fight against procrastination, don't get me wrong. It's frustrating, and it can be a real disability at times. But I've learned to embrace it, to harness it as a superpower when I need it most. Even right now, I know this book needs to be typed if it's ever going to be published and read by you. But the truth is, I've been writing this book for over five years—on paper, in my head, piecing it together bit by bit. And maybe that's just how my brain works best.

That Thursday night, just hours before the final project was due, I was handed a permission slip for a field trip. The class was headed to the state fairgrounds, and the catch? We weren't just showing our projects in class—we were submitting them to the Regional State Science Fair. Every single project was going to be judged by real scientists. I needed something, anything, good enough to pass. More than that, I just didn't want to look like the kid who threw something together overnight.

Before class ended, I asked the teacher how exactly we'd be graded. His response felt like both a lifeline and a warning: "If your project can show the judges that you put real time and energy into it, they'll be the ones who grade you. If you get a 3 out of 10, you'll pass." A 3. That was my goal. Not to impress anyone, not to stand out—just to survive this and move on.

What happened next still surprises me to this day. It's one of those moments that makes me incredibly proud of how my mind works under pressure.

I begged my mom to take me to the store that night. We didn't have much, but I needed something—anything—to start this project. She came home with a single piece of poster board, the only one left in stock. It was bright yellow. To top it off, she also picked up some yellow construction paper, a darker shade, assuming it might help with the project's "theme." When I saw it, I was stunned—and probably more than a little mean about it. *Yellow? Really?*

In hindsight, I know I hurt her feelings with my reaction. But I also know she was used to it by then, dealing with a kid like me. She didn't take it personally, even though she had every right to. I'm grateful for that. And honestly, I'm grateful for that yellow poster board too—the "pee paper," as I called it in my frustration.

What next? Well, staring at that bright yellow paper, the only thing that came to mind was pee. And that's when it hit me—if I leaned into the shock value and made my project about pee or something just as gross, maybe, just maybe, I could distract everyone from noticing how rushed and ridiculous the whole thing was. I figured if I could get a reaction, I might just squeak by with that 3 rating. Shock my way into a passing grade.

We had a computer at the time, but there was no way I knew how to type up anything, let alone print it out. This was the era when handwritten papers were still totally acceptable if printing wasn't an option. So, I scrounged around the house looking for any paper to write on. Of course, the only thing I could find was yellow legal paper. So now, the entire theme of my project was an overwhelming yellow. Perfect, right?

As I sat there, staring at all this yellow, I suddenly thought of my cat—Baby Kitty. She was an angry little Persian, mean as hell but with a soft spot for me. I loved her, even though she left me with more than a few scars over the years. Her favorite thing was to curl up on my chest, and God forbid I tried to move her—she'd scratch the life out of me. I miss that cat. But in that moment, I realized she was going to be the star of my project.

The shock value had to come from her. So, I decided to name my project "The Feces of a Cat." I spun an entire story about how I had been feeding Baby Kitty different types of canned food (true) and studying her poop each day (not entirely true). I claimed to have analyzed the different shapes, textures, and smells of her, uh, output. I even threw together a pie chart with percentages for my so-called "findings." I had no clue how to make a proper pie chart—it looked like something a kindergartener would put together. But I knew this wasn't about scientific accuracy. I just needed to pull off the shock.

I cut out the letters for the title from the darker yellow construction paper and glued them, along with my handwritten pages, onto the bright yellow poster board. The project was almost done, but it still needed something. I wasn't quite there yet. It needed that "cherry on top."

That's when it hit me: the feces. I needed actual cat poop to sell the story. So, I grabbed some of Baby Kitty's fresh poop, with a piece of tissue paper, and placed it in a small Tupperware container. That would be the ultimate distraction. My mom never saw the project—I kept it hidden from her because I knew she'd be horrified and would probably stop me from turning it in out of sheer embarrassment. But that was how I knew I was onto something. If even I was embarrassed, then I had probably nailed the shock value. I was sure now—I would at least pass.

The next morning, I remembered feeling nothing but excitement—no nerves, no fear—just pure thrill at the thought of having actual cat poop on display for everyone to see. I wasn't worried about failing;

I was more excited about the possibility of being sent to the principal's office for my little stunt. The project was folded up neatly, and the poop was safely stashed in my backpack the whole way to school.

When we arrived, we were guided to our spots to set up. I'll never forget seeing Becky, just five spots down, proudly wheeling in her suitcase full of supplies. She had this look of satisfaction, like she knew she was about to ace this thing. Even Matt's volcano looked impressive. I knew then that my only chance was to lean hard into the shock factor.

I waited until everyone had set up their projects and was called to assembly. I stayed behind, watching them file into the theater, and once the coast was clear, I set up my masterpiece. "The Feces of a Cat" was blindingly yellow, standing out in the sea of carefully crafted displays. Even if someone wanted to miss it, they couldn't. One of my notebook pages refused to lie flat, but I didn't care—at least it could still be read. I carefully placed the Tupperware container with Baby Kitty's "specimen" front and center, lid off, ready for all to see. With everything in place, I headed to join the assembly.

Once inside, we had to sit through student after student presenting their projects. Becky, of course, got called up to go over her solar system slides. She had clearly put in a ton of work, and when she won an award later, it was no surprise to anyone. She earned it. Meanwhile, I was sitting there, fingers crossed, just hoping my yellow display and "research" would somehow be enough for the judges to give me that magic 3 out of 10.

What I didn't realize was that while we were in the assembly—and later during lunch—the judges were reviewing all the projects, over 1,500 from our region, deciding the 1st, 2nd, and 3rd place winners. I was just praying not to fail.

At lunch, Becky passed by me and made a little jab: "You know, yellow is the first color the human eye sees, so at least the judges will notice how bad your project is." My mom always told me girls tease boys they like, but something told me Becky definitely didn't like me.

That comment stuck with me, though. Years later, when I learned about color theory and marketing, I found out she was right. Yellow really is one of the first colors that grabs attention. Now, whenever I use yellow with intention in my work or marketing, I think of Becky—and I thank her for that little factoid.

Like usual, when lunch let out and everyone headed back in to see who won and how their projects were rated, I hung near the back of the line. It's something I've always done—even now, I like to stand back and watch people. There's something about the way the room buzzes right after an event like this, and I love the quiet conversations with the staff that happen after everyone else has left. I remember a janitor giving me a nod and saying, "Break a leg," as I walked through the double doors.

Now, if you're anything like me, you've probably picked up on where this story is going.

As I rounded the corner, I noticed groups of students huddled around Matt's volcano and Becky's solar system. Both were surrounded by classmates congratulating them on their hard work. No one was near my project—which, considering the open container of cat poop, wasn't exactly shocking. But what did surprise me was the sight of a large trophy sitting in front of my display. It had this cool black base with psychedelic speckles and a small angel perched on top. The plaque at the bottom read "1st Place Winner," and there was a note taped below it. The note said, "Anyone this brave deserves 1st place," with a small "congrats" scribbled underneath and some initials I can't remember.

What happened next is something I will never forget. This rush of overwhelming excitement hit me, and I think I smiled bigger than I ever had in my life. I had never won anything before—not a trophy, not an award, nothing. I stood there in disbelief, trying to soak in the fact that I *had won*. My instinct was to turn and share that moment with someone, anyone. But when I looked up, the smiles and cheers around Matt and Becky had faded, replaced with looks of confusion—and maybe even a little resentment—directed at me.

That moment of joy quickly twisted into something else, something heavier. A weird mix of pride and loneliness washed over me. I still feel it, even now as I type this. It's one of those memories that stirs up emotions just as vividly as the day it happened. Do you ever get that? Can you recall something from years ago, and feel it all over again—like it consumes you for a moment, even late at night, when you're supposed to be sleeping?

For me, this is one of those moments. Even after all these years, it still sits with me—this blend of joy and sadness that lingers like an old bruise that never quite heals.

I tell you this, and what comes next, not to make you feel sorry for me. That's not the point. What I want is to share my thoughts, my feelings, and the realizations I've had that, until I met my very first autistic person, I thought belonged only to me. It's an isolating feeling, thinking you might be crazy or that what's going on in your head isn't something you can safely share with anyone. There's always that risk—if you open up, people might label you, distance themselves, or worse.

I know that some of you reading this for the first time know exactly what I'm talking about. You've felt that same fear of being misunderstood. And it wasn't until I learned there were so many others—thousands, millions—experiencing the same thing, or even worse, that I realized I had to share my story. Not for sympathy, but because I want the people who feel strange, weird, or abnormal to know there are others just like them. People like me.

Because the truth is, when enough of us embrace being "weird," it stops being weird. It just becomes normal. And really, what is normal, anyway? I've come to believe I'm not weird at all—I'm exceptional in many ways because of my differences. I wear that label of "weird" proudly now. It's not a flaw. It's a strength.

Enough rambling. Let's wrap up this story and get to the heart of this book!

After the awards were handed out, the science teacher came over to congratulate me. It was brief, and I could tell by his tone that he wasn't impressed—if anything, he seemed disgusted. He already didn't like me, and this win seemed to deepen whatever issue he had with me. The victory I thought would feel amazing... didn't. A lot of kids seemed disappointed, maybe because they felt their work was better. Becky ended up with some sort of ribbon, and Matt, well, he didn't win anything.

The bus ride home was unusually quiet. Matt never spoke to me again after that. He didn't even acknowledge me. He stopped sitting next to me in class and made it clear he was done with me. Becky, yet, had something to say the following Monday that would forever change my life.

At home, things were different. My mom and grandparents were thrilled. They saved the newspaper clipping with my picture (I didn't know it would be taken just yet); I found it years later in their keepsakes. I wish I'd held onto that trophy, but about 15 years later, in a moment of anger during one of those "clean it all out" days, I threw it away. I tossed out every award I'd ever earned, convinced none of it mattered. It's a decision I'll always regret.

But here's what I learned: just because something seems insignificant in the moment doesn't mean it won't hold meaning later. And that's a lesson I'll carry with me forever.

On Monday morning, still buzzing from the rare excitement at home, I headed to school with my backpack weighed down by the trophy I couldn't wait to show off. I was especially excited to share it with Stephanie. The whole weekend, I'd imagined pulling it out and seeing her smile. I thought for sure I'd walk in, and people would know, congratulate me, maybe even ask to see the trophy.

 But as I made my way through the first few classes, no one said a word. Not a single person mentioned it. That's when I started to realize that the science teacher hadn't shared my win with anyone. I walked past the front office, the place where I'd spent more time than in any classroom, said my usual hellos to the ladies behind the desk, and got the same polite but distant greeting in return. No recognition. No fanfare. Nothing.

 It became clear—I was not the celebrated student I thought I'd be. I mean, I'd won first place at a regional science fair for the school. Shouldn't that have meant something? As an adult, I still wonder if the teacher just forgot to mention it, was embarrassed by my project, or refused to say anything out of spite. I'll never know. But what I do know is that what happened next was the most hurtful, eye-opening moment of my life.

I rounded the corner to head into science class and saw Becky standing by the lockers with two of her friends and Matt. When she saw me, she smiled, and I took that as a good sign. I waved and said, "I heard you won an award too!" I started to take off my backpack, ready to pull out my trophy, but before I could, Becky's voice cut through the air.

"You only won because they felt sorry for you."

I froze, confused. "Felt sorry for me? What do you mean?"

With a smirk, she replied, "They only gave you first place because you're retarded. Everyone in the state knows you're a retard now."

Her friends giggled, and then they turned and walked into class, leaving me standing there, stunned. I couldn't speak. I fought back tears, but they were already welling up. I looked at Matt, hoping for something, but he just looked at me for a moment, his face showing a flicker of sympathy before he turned and walked inside, too.

Becky, though—she just stood there, staring at me with this growing smile on her face, like she was feeding off my pain. It felt like she was getting stronger as my sadness grew. I'll never forget her face, the way she seemed to revel in making me feel small. She didn't say another word, just turned around and walked into the classroom, letting the door close behind her.

Why would she say something like that? Was it because I volunteered in the special needs room? Did she really think less of me for helping kids who needed it? Her words hurt—deeply—but what hurt more was the thought that, in some twisted way, she was insulting not just me but the kids I had grown close to over the past year. It was a pain I didn't know how to process at the time, and honestly, one that still stings to this day.

I didn't go into that science room that day. Instead, I went straight to the one place I knew would make me feel better—the Special Needs room to see Stephanie.

As soon as Stephanie saw me, her whole face lit up, and she started bouncing in her chair, clapping her hands against the armrests. It was like she'd been waiting for me all day. The nurses, seeing her excitement, started clapping too, and the moment I walked in, I just broke down in tears. The nurse came over quickly and asked what was wrong. Through my tears, I told her that I thought no one cared about my win, that no one even knew.

She gave me this warm smile and said, "Oh honey, the front office just got a call from the newspaper! They want to come take a picture of you with your project!" That was the moment of joy I'd been hoping for all day, and it came from the people I cherished most—Stephanie and the rest of the kids in that room. Their excitement was real, and when I pulled out the trophy and told them the story behind it, their laughter filled the room. I even admitted to them—something I didn't dare tell anyone else—that I'd made up most of my project just to avoid failing.

The nurse just laughed and said, "Well, it'll be our little secret," and we all laughed so hard that tears rolled down our faces and our sides ached. It was pure happiness. I never mentioned what Becky had said. It didn't seem to matter in that room. Later, as my picture was taken for the paper, Stephanie and the nurse stood in the front office, waving and cheering me on. That was the joy I had been waiting for—the validation from people who actually cared about me.

That night, when my mom got home from work, I told her all about the great moments from my day. I was beaming with pride as I shared the highlight—knowing that I'd be in the paper! But, as if my excitement had an end date, it started to fade quickly, and the memory of Becky's cruel words came rushing back. I felt the weight of it all hit me, and I started tearing up.

My mom noticed right away and asked what was wrong. I told her about what Becky said, how she called me "retarded" and said I only won because they felt sorry for me. I tried to explain that it hurt worse because I loved volunteering to help the kids in the Special Needs room—it was something I genuinely enjoyed.

That's when everything changed. My entire life shifted in that moment.

My mom looked at me and said, "Oh Joey, I'm sorry I never told you, it's probably because you're not just volunteering for that class—you're in the class." I stared at her, not understanding what she meant. She continued, "The school told me you might have something like Attention Deficit Disorder, or the other one with hyperactivity, but they weren't sure. So, they came up with a plan to help you with your grades and other things."

I can't quite describe the feeling that washed over me then. It was like being caught between lightheadedness and passing out. My skin prickled with pins and needles, and I felt this heavy shame settle over me. The word "retarded" echoed in my head. I looked at my mom and asked, "Am I retarded? Did my trophy even count, or was it just a special one?"

She looked at me with all the love a mother could give and said, "No, no, honey. That trophy was real, and it was something special. You're not retarded. People who use those words to hurt others are the ones with a problem. You're special—special in ways that help you do things others can't even understand.

I don't even fully understand, but you're not what they say you are."

Her words were kind, but they couldn't quite erase the confusion and hurt I felt. It was like my world had tilted on its axis, and I was just starting to understand what that meant.

I was special. I was unique, and in that moment, I realized that it didn't matter whether Becky liked me. I had won fair and square. What hit me then, and something I understand even more now, is that whether you're neurotypical or neurodiverse, the world can be a cruel place. No matter how much you win or achieve, there will always be someone hoping for your downfall. That's just the way things are. As much as I've wished for the world to be kinder or easier to navigate, I've come to accept that some things don't change. But here's the thing: I don't have to let that crush me.

Perhaps the biggest lesson I've learned from being autistic—diagnosed many years later—is that there are certain things I'll never fully understand, like why people are so quick to tear others down. But I've also learned that I can adapt. I can embrace the fact that these "unwritten rules" exist and work to soften the impact they have on me. After all, life isn't about what happens to me; it's about how I respond to it. That's something I've held onto.

I *am* weird. I *am* different. But more importantly, I am exceptional. And that's what neurodiversity has taught me—it's not just about being different for the sake of being different. It's about seeing those differences as strengths, even when the world doesn't. Neurodiversity is becoming more widely recognized now, and it's starting to become the "norm" to embrace these differences. If I can use my experiences to help even one person understand and embrace their own uniqueness, then maybe I can help soften the rough and brutal moments that inevitably shape us.

Because the truth is, the world isn't always kind. But that doesn't mean we can't be kind to ourselves. And if we can do that—if we can embrace who we are, no matter how weird or different we feel—then maybe the world starts to make a little more sense. At least, that's what I hope.

Photo Courtesy of Jay Aldrich

A note to all readers,

As you read this book, I invite you to reflect on your own journey—whether you identify as neurodiverse or not. We all have differences that set us apart, but it's how we embrace those differences that defines us. If you've ever felt like the world wasn't built for someone like you, you're not alone. My hope is that my story helps you see that being different isn't just okay—it's what makes you exceptional.

The world can be tough, but we all have the power to rise above it. By embracing who you are—quirks, challenges, and all—you can open doors you never thought possible. This book is proof that thriving despite the labels and judgments isn't just possible, it's inevitable when you own your uniqueness. Together, we can redefine what it means to be "normal."

Together we can be exceptional.

EMBRACING NEURODIVERGENCE STARTS WITH UNDERSTANDING

Chapter 1

The world likes to tell us what's "normal." We're constantly fed this image of what a typical life should look like—how we should think, behave, work, and interact with others. The message is clear: fit in, don't stand out, follow the rules. But for many of us who are neurodivergent, "normal" was never an option.

Maybe you've felt this way, too. You might have sensed from an early age that you don't quite see the world the same way others do. Perhaps you've struggled to fit into environments that demand you be someone you're not—sitting still in classrooms, working quietly in offices, engaging in small talk at parties. These expectations might have made you feel like you're constantly missing the mark, like you're broken in some way.

But what if the problem isn't with you? What if the system itself is flawed, designed with a narrow idea of what it means to be functional or successful?

Neurodivergence—whether you're autistic, have ADHD, are dyslexic, or possess any number of other cognitive variations—isn't about being broken. It's about having a brain that works differently. And different doesn't mean worse. In fact, those differences are often the very traits that give neurodivergent individuals their greatest strengths. The key is learning to understand how your brain works, so you can embrace what makes you unique and thrive on your own terms.

This chapter is the starting point on your journey toward self-awareness and empowerment. You'll learn what I think neurodivergence really is, explore the diverse landscape of different neurotypes, and begin to dismantle the harmful myths that have likely shaped your experience up until now. But most importantly, this is where you'll start to recognize that your neurodivergence is not a flaw; it's a strength.

The path ahead won't always be easy—self-acceptance rarely is—but it's a path worth taking. Because once you stop trying to fit into a world that wasn't built for you, you can start creating your own world. And that's when the magic happens.

The Landscape of Neurodivergence: Diverse Minds, Diverse Strengths

Neurodivergence isn't a single condition or label. It's a broad term that covers a range of cognitive differences—each with its own unique set of strengths, challenges, and ways of processing the world. To truly embrace your neurodivergent identity, it's important to first understand the variety that exists within this spectrum. Whether you already know your specific neurotype or are still figuring it out, learning about the landscape of neurodivergence will give you the clarity and confidence you need to move forward. If you're looking to focus on and understand the disability aspect of neurodiversity, this book will not be what you're seeking—there are many other options for that focus aside from this book.

What Is Neurodivergence?

At its core, neurodivergence refers to brains that diverge from the neurotypical norm. Neurotypical individuals are those whose cognitive functioning aligns with societal expectations of "normal" thought patterns, learning styles, and behavior. In contrast, neurodivergent individuals experience the world differently. They might think faster or slower, focus deeply on topics others find trivial, struggle with traditional learning methods, or excel in creative problem-solving while facing challenges in other areas.

The term "neurodivergent" was coined in the late 1990s by sociologist Judy Singer, who wanted to shift the conversation from seeing cognitive differences as disorders to understanding them as natural variations of the human brain. This was revolutionary because, for most of history, people who didn't fit into the narrow definition of "normal" were treated as though something was wrong with them. Singer's neurodiversity paradigm has helped change that. It encouraged society to see these differences not as deficits, but as part of the rich diversity that makes us human. But society still has a long way to go to achieving acceptance.

The Different Types of Neurodivergence

Let's break down the major types of neurodivergence you may already be familiar with, or may be part of your own experience:

Autism Spectrum Disorder (ASD): Autism is often characterized by differences in social communication, sensory sensitivity, and a tendency toward deep, focused interests. Autistic people may have heightened sensory experiences, finding lights too bright or sounds too overwhelming. They often thrive on routine and find comfort in order. What others see as a lack of social skills may, in fact, be a different way of connecting—one that values honesty, directness, and loyalty over small talk and superficial interaction. Some autistic individuals are brilliant at identifying patterns, thinking in innovative ways, and approaching problems with fresh perspectives.

Attention-Deficit/Hyperactivity Disorder (ADHD): ADHD is typically associated with challenges in focus, impulsivity, and hyperactivity. But what's often overlooked is the *hyperfocus* that many people with ADHD experience. When fully engaged in a task they're passionate about, individuals with ADHD can work with incredible intensity and creativity. Their brains are wired for spontaneity and can come up with brilliant solutions that others might miss. While traditional work environments might see ADHD as a hurdle, people with ADHD often excel in fast-paced, dynamic situations where they can constantly switch gears and think on their feet.

Dyslexia: Dyslexia primarily affects reading and writing skills, but it comes with a host of compensatory strengths. Many dyslexic individuals have exceptional spatial reasoning and excel in creative fields like design, architecture, and engineering. They think in pictures rather than words, which gives them a distinct advantage in seeing the big picture when others get bogged down in details. In fact, many of the world's greatest innovators—from Steve Jobs to Richard Branson—are dyslexic, proving that traditional literacy skills are just one measure of intelligence.

Dyspraxia: Dyspraxia affects motor skills and coordination, often making tasks that require fine motor skills, like handwriting or sports, difficult. But dyspraxic individuals tend to be excellent at strategic thinking, long-term planning, and emotional intelligence. Their brains are wired to think several steps ahead, which can make them natural leaders and problem-solvers. Their challenge with physical coordination is balanced by their ability to navigate complex cognitive and social environments with ease.

Tourette Syndrome: Tourette's is often characterized by involuntary movements or sounds, known as tics. What's less known is that individuals with Tourette's often have heightened sensory awareness and rapid decision-making skills. They can process information at lightning speed and adapt quickly to changing situations. People with

Tourette's often develop a deep understanding of self-regulation and empathy for others, particularly when it comes to navigating difficult social dynamics.

There are many MANY others but we will list more in a later chapter––don't worry, if you aren't represented above I'm certain you will feel represented as we continue. You can skip ahead to chapter 6 where I dive into all of the types of diversities I have made note of over the years.

Why did I list these types? We're just getting started and I chose the most common known types. I also knew it was too early in the book to dive much deeper so I decided a reference to the later chapter was the best possible way to support all readers.

The Overlap of Strengths and Challenges

One thing you'll notice as you explore these different types of neurodivergence is that there's no clear line between strengths and challenges—they often coexist in complex ways. For instance:

- **ADHD** can make focusing on a mundane task feel impossible, but it also fuels intense bursts of creative energy.

- **Autism** might make navigating social interactions difficult, but it can also sharpen focus and bring incredible depth to areas of interest.

Each neurotype comes with its own unique balance of gifts and hurdles. The key is to recognize where your strengths lie and where you might need extra support—not to see these challenges as personal failings, but as opportunities to understand yourself better.

Understanding the Spectrum

It's important to note that neurodivergence exists on a spectrum. Even within a single neurotype like autism or ADHD, there's a wide range of experiences. No two people experience their neurodivergence in exactly the same way. You might find that some descriptions resonate deeply with you, while others don't. That's okay. Part of embracing your neurodivergence is learning to define it for yourself, rather than letting someone else's definition limit you.

Take time to reflect on how these descriptions align with your experiences. Does your ADHD show up in bursts of creativity and frustration with routines? Does your autism manifest as deep focus and a need for structure? Understanding the landscape of neurodivergence helps you see how your mind works and, more importantly, how you can start using that knowledge to your advantage.

As you learn about the different types of neurodivergence and begin to see where you fit, remember that this is just the starting point. The goal here isn't to label yourself but to better understand how your brain operates. Once you do, you'll be better equipped to harness its strengths, anticipate its challenges, and navigate the world on your own terms. You're not here to fit into someone else's definition of normal—you're here to redefine what exceptional looks like for yourself.

Strengths and Challenges: Reframing Your Neurodivergence

By now, you've likely begun to recognize that your neurodivergence is not simply a set of "symptoms" or a list of deficits. It's a different way of processing the world, and with that comes a unique blend of strengths and challenges. The key to embracing your neurodivergence isn't just about managing what's difficult; it's about reframing how you see those difficulties and recognizing that your strengths come from the very same place.

Previously we explored the landscape of neurodivergence and how different neurotypes—such as ADHD, autism, and dyslexia—have their own distinct traits. What we often overlook, though, is how closely those strengths are intertwined with the challenges. The goal here is to help you see both sides of that coin and to start thinking of your challenges not as barriers to success, but as parts of a bigger picture—one where your strengths can truly shine.

Recognizing the Duality of Traits

One of the first steps to reframing your neurodivergence is recognizing the duality in many of the traits associated with it. What might feel like a burden in certain situations can also be your greatest asset in others. Let's break this down into some practical examples:

Autistic Focus vs. Overwhelm: Autistic individuals are often praised for their ability to focus deeply on topics that interest them. This is sometimes referred to as *hyperfocus*—an intense immersion in a task or area of interest that can lead to groundbreaking insights or mastery of complex subjects. But this strength often comes with a flip side: sensory overwhelm and a need for strict routines. When the world doesn't cooperate with that focus—when noise, unpredictability, or social demands disrupt the calm—it can feel like everything is spiraling out of control.

The challenge, then, isn't about "curing" the overwhelm or forcing yourself to be more flexible. Instead, it's about finding environments and structures where your ability to hyperfocus can thrive. Ask yourself: *When do I feel most at peace? When am I at my most productive and engaged?* Once you identify those conditions, you can start advocating for them in your daily life—whether that's requesting noise-canceling headphones at work or blocking off time to work on passion projects uninterrupted. Your focus is a gift, and your need for routine isn't a flaw—it's the foundation that allows that gift to flourish.

ADHD Creativity vs. Impulsivity: People with ADHD are often recognized for their spontaneity, creativity, and ability to think outside the box. These traits come from the same place as impulsivity and distractibility. It's the ADHD brain's tendency to jump from idea to idea that creates new, exciting connections, but it's also what can make it hard to sit down and finish a task. You might have experienced the thrill of starting multiple projects only to feel paralyzed when it comes time to complete them.

The trick here is to reframe impulsivity as an *asset* rather than a liability. Your quick, nonlinear thinking is what allows you to solve problems that others can't, but that doesn't mean you have to fight the structure forever. Create systems that honor your impulsive nature—like having multiple projects going at once, so you can bounce between them—and use tools like timers or accountability partners to bring focus when needed. The goal isn't to suppress the impulsivity but to channel it into creativity without letting it derail your progress.

Dyslexic Problem-Solving vs. Traditional Learning Struggles: Dyslexia is often seen through the lens of difficulty with reading and writing, but that's an incomplete picture. Dyslexic individuals frequently excel at big-picture thinking and creative problem-solving, often able to approach problems from angles others miss entirely. They're natural visual thinkers and have a strong ability to see how different pieces of a puzzle fit together.

On the flip side, traditional educational environments can feel suffocating—where success is defined by literacy and memorization. If you're dyslexic, you might have spent years feeling like you were constantly behind, even though your mind was probably working at full capacity—just in a different way. The challenge here is to recognize that your difficulties with reading don't define your intelligence. In fact, they highlight the gap between how schools teach and how you learn best. Your visual thinking and ability to connect seemingly unrelated ideas can be invaluable in fields like design, engineering, and entrepreneurship, where innovation is key.

Turning Challenges Into Opportunities

Once you begin to see the duality in your traits, the next step is learning how to *leverage* those challenges as opportunities for growth and success. Here's how you can start to do that:

Shift Your Mindset from "Problem" to "Pattern": Instead of viewing your challenges as isolated issues, start looking for patterns in how and when they appear. For example, if you know that sensory overwhelm strikes in noisy, chaotic environments, you can begin to avoid or adapt to those environments—by working from home, using calming sensory tools, or taking regular breaks. Once you see the pattern, you can build strategies around it.

This pattern recognition isn't just about avoiding discomfort; it's about building a life that *works for you*. The world may not always bend to meet your needs, but you can certainly start designing a life where your neurodivergence is a strength, not a barrier. I know because I work towards this every single day–some days are easier than others.

Practice Strategic Self-Acceptance: Accepting your challenges doesn't mean resigning yourself to them. It means being honest about what you need to thrive. Self-acceptance is about recognizing where your neurodivergence makes certain tasks more difficult and allowing yourself the grace to ask for help when you need it. For instance, using assistive technology for dyslexia or working in short bursts if you have ADHD isn't about "giving up"—it's about leaning into tools that empower you to perform at your best.

Strategic self-acceptance also means letting go of the pressure to be good at everything. Society often pushes neurodivergent people to "fix" their weaknesses rather than celebrating their strengths. But what if, instead of trying to force yourself to fit into a mold that was never designed for you, you focused on amplifying your natural gifts? Imagine what you could achieve if you were allowed to *be yourself* unapologetically.

Reframe "Failure" as Insight: Neurodivergent people often struggle with perfectionism, in part because we've been conditioned to think that we need to work twice as hard to be seen as competent. But the reality is, failure isn't something to be avoided—it's a powerful teacher. When you struggle with something, it's not a sign that you're inadequate. It's information. It's feedback that shows you where your current strategies might need tweaking or where external systems aren't built to support you.

Embracing failure as part of your process allows you to experiment without fear. If a certain work environment doesn't suit your needs, it doesn't mean you're not capable—it just means that environment isn't designed for how you thrive. Seek out or create environments that support your neurodivergence. When you stop seeing failure as a personal indictment, you free yourself to take risks, and with those risks come greater rewards.

Playing to Your Strengths

We often talk about strengths and weaknesses as if they're separate, but as you've likely realized by now, they're deeply connected. Once you stop trying to hide or compensate for your challenges, you can begin to focus on what you're *naturally good at*. Here are a few ways to harness those strengths:

Leverage Your Hyperfocus: If you have autism or ADHD, you might experience periods of intense focus when working on something you're passionate about. Use this to your advantage by structuring your time in a way that maximizes these moments. When you're in a flow state, don't interrupt yourself—ride the wave of productivity. If your focus is sporadic, that's okay too. Schedule work during your peak hours and allow yourself the freedom to rest when you're not in that state of mind. It's ok to NOT do anything! Sometimes nothing, is the preparation we need to accomplish everything.

Embrace Creative Problem-Solving: Neurodivergent individuals are known for their innovative approaches to problem-solving. Whether you're designing, writing, coding, or managing a team, you can bring a unique perspective that others might miss. Don't shy away from thinking differently—in fact, double down on it. When faced with a challenge, ask yourself: *What if I approached this from a completely new angle?* Trust that your brain's natural creativity is its own superpower.

Develop Emotional Resilience: Many neurodivergent people develop resilience as a result of navigating a world that wasn't built for them. You've likely had to learn how to adapt, cope, and bounce back from setbacks in ways others haven't. This emotional resilience is one of your greatest strengths. It gives you the ability to persevere, to find unconventional solutions, and to empathize with others who struggle. This resilience will carry you through the moments when things feel difficult or overwhelming.

Recognizing the strengths and challenges of your neurodivergence is a powerful first step in reframing how you see yourself. The very traits that make some tasks difficult are also the traits that make you exceptional. Embracing this duality is key to understanding that your challenges aren't obstacles.

The Uncharted Territory of Neurodivergence: Beyond the Well-Known Types

While we've covered some of the more commonly recognized types of neurodivergence, such as autism, ADHD, and dyslexia, the truth is, the landscape of neurodivergence is far more vast and intricate than most people realize. In fact, there are many neurodivergent traits and conditions that haven't been fully classified or studied in-depth yet. These lesser-known neurotypes often go undiagnosed or misunderstood, leading individuals to believe they're alone in their experiences.

The reason? A lot of neurodivergent individuals feel uncomfortable or afraid to speak openly about these traits, fearing they might sound strange or be dismissed as "made up." As a result, many of these neurotypes remain on the fringes of public awareness, with little research allocated to them. But the more people share their experiences, the clearer it becomes that these neurodivergent differences are not rare quirks—they're foundational to how many people experience the world.

Here are some of the lesser-known types of neurodivergence that are slowly gaining recognition:

Synesthesia

Synesthesia is a fascinating condition in which the senses overlap, leading to experiences like *seeing sounds* or *tasting colors.* For example, someone with synesthesia might associate specific colors with certain numbers or letters, or they might hear music and simultaneously experience visual patterns or colors. This is not imagination or magic—it's a real, consistent sensory phenomenon, deeply embedded in the individual's perception of the world.

Chromesthesia

Chromesthesia is a subtype of synesthesia where sounds automatically evoke the perception of colors. Many people with chromesthesia describe music or everyday sounds as creating a visual display of colors, shapes, or light. Far from being a distraction, some find it enhances creativity—many artists and musicians have reported this condition.

Aphantasia and Hyperphantasia

Both of these conditions relate to the vividness (or lack thereof) of mental imagery:

Aphantasia is the inability to form mental images. If you were to ask someone with aphantasia to imagine a beach, they wouldn't be able to "see" it in their mind's eye, even though they might conceptually understand what a beach looks like.

Hyperphantasia, on the other hand, is the opposite—individuals with this trait have an exceptionally vivid imagination, capable of producing extremely detailed mental images. They can summon complex, immersive scenes in their mind with clarity that rivals real life.

For years, people with aphantasia were often left confused when told to "picture" something, and many didn't even realize their brain was processing things differently. Similarly, those with hyperphantasia might have kept their vivid imaginations to themselves, fearing they were seen as overly dramatic. Yet these traits are deeply tied to how these individuals navigate daily life, approach problem-solving, and relate to their environments.

Obsessive-Compulsive Disorder (OCD)

OCD is often misrepresented in popular culture as just an obsession with cleanliness or order. In reality, it's far more complex. People with OCD experience intrusive, often distressing thoughts (obsessions) that compel them to engage in certain behaviors or rituals (compulsions) to ease the anxiety these thoughts cause.

While OCD is technically classified as a mental health disorder, it shares many characteristics with neurodivergence, particularly in the way it alters thinking patterns, attention to detail, and behaviors. Many neurodivergent people with OCD have found their hyper-focus and meticulousness to be both a challenge and a unique strength when channeled into the right environments.

Oppositional Defiant Disorder (ODD)

ODD is characterized by chronic, ongoing defiance, anger, and irritability, often directed at authority figures. While this condition is typically diagnosed in childhood, its effects can extend well into adulthood, manifesting as difficulty with following traditional hierarchies or routines. People with ODD tend to resist being told what to do or how to do it, which can create friction in traditional work or educational settings. However, this same trait can make them highly independent thinkers who thrive in environments that value autonomy and creativity.

Other Emerging Neurotypes:

There are several other forms of neurodivergence that are just beginning to gain recognition. These include:

Misophonia: A strong emotional reaction, often anger or anxiety, triggered by specific sounds (like chewing or tapping). Individuals with misophonia can feel overwhelmed in environments with repetitive sounds, but they often have heightened auditory awareness, making them attuned to nuances others might miss.

Sensory Processing Disorder (SPD): Some individuals experience heightened or diminished sensitivity to sensory input—whether it's light, sound, touch, taste, or smell. This can lead to sensory overload in busy environments or the need for strong sensory stimuli to feel comfortable. People with SPD are often highly attuned to subtle changes in their environment, which can be an asset in certain situations.

Prosopagnosia (Face Blindness): This condition makes it difficult or impossible to recognize faces, even of people the individual knows well. While it might sound like a serious hindrance (and it can be in social contexts), many people with prosopagnosia develop remarkable compensatory skills—such as recognizing others through their voice, body language, or other unique markers.

Why These Neurotypes Remain Under-Discussed

So why have these forms of neurodivergence remained so under-discussed and under-researched? Part of the reason is that many people who experience these traits have been conditioned to feel that their experiences are "weird" or "unbelievable." They may fear being dismissed or not taken seriously if they open up about their experiences. After all, how do you explain to someone that you literally *see* sound or *can't imagine* a visual scene in your head without feeling like they might doubt your reality?

As a result, many adults who live with these conditions keep them to themselves, afraid that talking about them will invite ridicule or confusion. But the more we open up about these experiences, the more we start to see just how common they are. Neurodivergent people often feel isolated in their unique experiences because society hasn't made space for them—but the reality is, many of these traits are shared across large groups of people.

The hypothesis here is simple: **when neurodivergent people feel safe enough to share the full spectrum of their experiences, we will begin to see how many of these traits are more common than we've ever realized.** It's not that these neurotypes are rare—it's that we haven't been talking about them enough. And once we start these conversations, we can push for the research and support systems that neurodivergent individuals deserve.

Encouraging Openness and Research

The more we share about these lesser-known neurotypes, the more we validate those who live with them. Adults who feel capable of opening up about their experiences are paving the way for others who may have been hiding these parts of themselves out of fear. As these conversations become more common, we'll not only reduce the stigma but also drive research into these areas—research that will help us better understand the full scope of neurodivergence and how to support neurodivergent individuals in thriving, no matter how their brains are wired.

It's time to shift the narrative. These experiences—whether it's seeing colors when you hear music or struggling to recognize a familiar face—aren't "weird" or "fake." They're real, they matter, and they're a core part of what makes people who they are. Embracing these traits means embracing the fullness of your neurodivergence, and in doing so, you empower others to do the same.

As we explore these lesser-known types of neurodivergence, it becomes clear that the world has only begun to scratch the surface of understanding how diverse human brains truly are. Whether classified or not, these neurotypes shape how people experience and interact with the world. The more we talk about them, the more we'll start to see just how interconnected and widespread these experiences really are. By opening up about these traits, we pave the way for others to do the same, creating a future where no one feels like their neurodivergence is something to hide.

Turning Challenges into Opportunities: Reframing Your Experience

If you've made it this far, you're already beginning to understand that neurodivergence comes with a unique set of strengths and challenges. But this section is about taking it a step further. It's about **actively reframing** those challenges, seeing them not just as obstacles to overcome but as springboards for growth and success. This is where we move from understanding your neurodivergence to *owning* it—embracing your differences as powerful assets that can propel you forward in ways you may not have imagined.

While the world may not always be designed with neurodivergent individuals in mind, that doesn't mean you have to play by its rules. In fact, many of the most innovative thinkers, creators, and leaders in history didn't fit the mold either. What they had in common was their ability to turn their neurodivergent traits—both the strengths and the struggles—into opportunities.

The Power of Reframing

Reframing is the process of looking at a situation, trait, or challenge through a different lens. It's about shifting the way you view your neurodivergence, from seeing it as something to be fixed or hidden, to recognizing it as an integral part of who you are—one that can lead to success on your terms.

Let's be real for a moment: the world can be exhausting for neurodivergent individuals. Schools, workplaces, and social environments are often built around neurotypical norms, leaving you feeling like you're constantly swimming upstream. But here's the truth: **those environments don't define you.**

The moment you shift your perspective and stop comparing yourself to neurotypical standards, you gain the freedom to see your challenges differently. The very traits that may have felt like barriers—your inability to sit still in class, your sensory sensitivities, your struggle with linear thinking—are the same traits that can drive creativity, innovation, and deep, meaningful work.

Learning to Play to Your Strengths

Each type of neurodivergence comes with its own set of strengths, as we've discussed in the previous sections. Now, it's time to identify how you can *actively harness* those strengths in a way that transforms your challenges into opportunities. Here's how:

Autism: Pattern Recognition as a Superpower If you're on the autism spectrum, you've likely noticed that you have an incredible ability to spot patterns, see connections, and think deeply about topics that others might gloss over. This strength is invaluable in fields like science, technology, mathematics, and even art.

But you might also find that this intense focus can make it hard to switch gears when the world demands something different. Here's where reframing comes in: instead of seeing your need for routine and structure as a limitation, think of it as the foundation that allows your deep thinking to thrive.

Opportunity: Seek out roles or environments that value deep focus, attention to detail, and problem-solving over quick multitasking. Whether it's data analysis, design, or programming, your ability to zero in on complex issues will make you stand out. Advocate for quiet workspaces, flexible hours, or other accommodations that enhance your productivity. Remember: you don't need to conform to a fast-paced environment to excel—you need to create conditions where your brain operates at its best.

ADHD: Harnessing Creativity and Energy

ADHD often gets framed as a disorder of attention and impulsivity. But if you look at it through a different lens, it's really a brain wired for creativity and rapid idea generation. While traditional work structures—like long meetings or rigid schedules—can feel suffocating, the flexibility to jump between tasks and follow your interests can lead to groundbreaking ideas and projects.

Opportunity: Reframe your impulsivity as **adaptability**. You're naturally inclined to think outside the box, which makes you a valuable asset in creative industries, fast-paced work environments, and roles that require innovative problem-solving.

Instead of trying to force yourself into a traditional mold, look for ways to build your work or daily schedule around how you operate best. Break your day into smaller, dynamic chunks, and give yourself permission to take creative detours. These are where some of your best ideas will come from.

Dyslexia: Seeing the Bigger Picture Dyslexia is often associated with difficulty in reading and writing, but this trait comes with extraordinary strengths in visual and spatial reasoning. If you're dyslexic, you're likely someone who can think in 3D, seeing how systems, ideas, or designs come together in ways others might miss. While school might have emphasized literacy as the ultimate skill, in the real world, your ability to visualize and innovate is far more valuable.

Opportunity: Reframe your struggle with traditional learning as **mastery in problem-solving and creative thinking**. Fields like architecture, design, and engineering thrive on the big-picture thinking dyslexic individuals often excel at. Don't waste time trying to conform to the minutiae—find opportunities where your ability to innovate, visualize, and think holistically can shine.

Creating Environments That Work for You

A critical part of turning challenges into opportunities is realizing that you don't have to conform to environments that weren't built for you. In fact, you can **design** environments—both physical and social—that allow your neurodivergence to flourish.

Sensory-Friendly Spaces: Whether you're autistic, have sensory processing disorder (SPD), or are simply more sensitive to stimuli, the world can be an overwhelming place. Reframe your sensitivity as a **gift for detail**. You notice things others don't—subtle changes in mood, the energy of a room, small design flaws that need fixing. But to use this gift, you need to be in spaces that don't overwhelm you.

Action Step: Advocate for sensory-friendly workspaces. If you work in a busy office, request noise-canceling headphones or a quieter room. If bright lights are a problem, ask for adjustable lighting. These small adjustments can make a world of difference in how you process information and perform tasks. And if you're building a business or creative space of your own, use your heightened sensory awareness to create an environment that feels *right* for you.

Flexible Schedules and Nonlinear Thinking: Neurodivergent brains often don't follow the 9-to-5, linear path that neurotypical society favors. Instead of seeing your inability to work within these constraints as a weakness, see it as a signal that **you're wired for something different.** Maybe you work best in bursts of intense focus, followed by periods of rest. Maybe you need to start your day later or work from home to be at your best.

Action Step: If you're in a position to negotiate, push for flexible hours that align with your natural rhythm. If you're in a creative field or an entrepreneur, build systems that allow for fluidity rather than rigidity. And if you don't yet have that flexibility, experiment with ways to maximize your focus and energy within your existing schedule. Reframe your need for flexibility as a **strategic advantage**—you're learning to work *with* your brain, not against it.

Overcoming Fear of Failure: Turning Setbacks into Growth

One of the greatest barriers neurodivergent individuals face is the **fear of failure**. After years of being told we're "doing it wrong" or that we're not living up to neurotypical standards, it's easy to internalize a belief that failure is inevitable—or worse, that it defines us. But here's the thing: **failure is inevitable for everyone**. The difference is that neurodivergent people can use their unique strengths to turn failures into powerful lessons for growth.

Failure as Feedback: When something doesn't go as planned, it's not a reflection of your worth or abilities. It's feedback. It's telling you what didn't work in a particular environment or under a specific set of conditions. This is true for neurotypical people as well, but neurodivergent individuals often get less room to fail without judgment. Give yourself permission to **fail forward**. Each failure brings with it valuable information about how your brain operates best—and that's gold.

Perseverance as a Superpower: Neurodivergent individuals are some of the most resilient people you'll meet. You've had to navigate a world that often wasn't built for you, and in doing so, you've built a well of **perseverance**. This resilience is a tool that allows you to try, fail, adapt, and try again. It's why so many successful entrepreneurs, artists, and creators are neurodivergent—they've learned how to turn obstacles into opportunities through sheer determination and creative thinking.

Supporting the Lesser-Known Neurotypes

As we discussed previously, there are many neurotypes—like synesthesia, misophonia, and aphantasia—that haven't received the same level of attention or research as more well-known conditions. But if you fall into one of these categories, you have a unique perspective and experience that deserves recognition.

When you find yourself feeling unseen or unsupported, remember this: **your neurodivergence is real, even if it doesn't have a well-defined label.** The world is still catching up to understanding these experiences, but that doesn't mean your reality is any less valid. As more people come forward to share their experiences, the body of knowledge will grow, and so will the support systems available to you.

Opportunity: Use your unique perspective to **educate and advocate** for yourself and others. If you experience something like chromesthesia or hyperphantasia, share that with your peers, your work environments, and your support systems. The more these neurotypes are discussed openly, the more normalized they become. You can be part of the movement that pushes for greater understanding and acceptance of all neurotypes.

Turning challenges into opportunities is not about denying the difficulties that come with neurodivergence. It's about recognizing that within those challenges lie the seeds of your greatest strengths. The world may not always be set up to accommodate your neurodivergence, but that doesn't mean you have to shrink to fit into it. By reframing your traits, creating environments that work for you, and embracing the resilience you've built, you can not only survive in a neurotypical world—you can thrive in ways that are uniquely your own.

Navigating the Neurotypical Bias: Thriving in a World Not Built for You

Let's face it: the world wasn't designed with neurodivergent individuals in mind. From childhood to adulthood, we're taught to conform to a narrow standard of thinking, behavior, and success—one that prioritizes linear, methodical, and often rigid ways of processing information. Neurotypical norms are baked into everything from how schools are structured to the way workplaces operate. If you've ever felt out of place in these environments, it's not your imagination.

The good news? You don't have to fit into this mold to succeed. In fact, by understanding where the system doesn't serve you and learning how to strategically advocate for yourself, you can carve out a space that works for you within this framework—or better yet, create a new one entirely.

Recognizing the Neurotypical Bias

The first step in navigating a world built on neurotypical assumptions is recognizing when and where these biases are present. You've probably encountered many of them throughout your life, though you might not have known what to call them at the time.

Consider the following:

Education Systems: Traditional education is often structured around the idea that students should sit still, follow directions, and absorb information presented in a linear, step-by-step manner. This leaves many neurodivergent students—especially those with ADHD or dyslexia—feeling frustrated, bored, or even like failures. But that's not a reflection of their intelligence or capability; it's a reflection of an outdated system that only works for a narrow range of learning styles.

Workplaces: The corporate world often values traits like multitasking, conformity, and strong verbal communication skills. Yet, for someone on the autism spectrum, for instance, these expectations might feel overwhelming or unnatural. The insistence on group projects, open-plan offices, and networking events can be draining rather than energizing for neurodivergent individuals.

Social Norms: Society places heavy emphasis on certain forms of communication, like making eye contact, engaging in small talk, and responding to unspoken social cues. For many neurodivergent people—especially those with autism or social anxiety—these norms can feel alienating or even impossible to navigate. The idea that there's one "right" way to engage with others creates unnecessary pressure and leaves many feeling excluded.

Recognizing these biases for what they are—limitations of a system, not personal flaws—is empowering. The more you understand that these structures were built with neurotypicals in mind, the less you'll feel like you're somehow "doing it wrong." Instead, you can begin to see where you need to advocate for changes that will allow you to thrive.

Advocating for Yourself Strategically

Advocacy doesn't have to be an uphill battle. You have the right to ask for accommodations and to create an environment that allows your neurodivergence to shine. Here's how you can start:

Know What Works for You: The first step in advocating for yourself is knowing what you need. This means understanding both your strengths and your challenges. For example, if you work best in a quiet, distraction-free environment, and your office is an open-plan space with constant noise, you have a legitimate reason to ask for a quieter workspace. Similarly, if you need more time to process written instructions due to dyslexia, it's reasonable to request deadlines that account for this.

Speak Up Early and Often: Don't wait until you're overwhelmed or burnt out to advocate for your needs. Whether you're in school, at work, or navigating social relationships, it's important to communicate your needs upfront. When you're clear about how your brain works and what you need to perform at your best, people are more likely to be receptive and accommodating.

Example: If you're starting a new job and know that sensory overload is a challenge for you, have a conversation with your supervisor about accommodations before it becomes an issue. You might request noise-canceling headphones, a desk in a quieter area, or flexibility to take breaks when you need them.

Frame Your Needs as Strengths: Advocacy is most effective when you frame your needs as an asset rather than a problem to be fixed. For instance, if you need longer blocks of uninterrupted time to focus because of ADHD, you can explain that this allows you to enter a hyperfocused state where you produce your best work. If you need to avoid unnecessary meetings, explain that your deep, independent work produces high-quality outcomes.

Example: "I know I work best when I have extended time to focus on a task without interruptions. If I can work from home one day a week, I can be more productive and deliver better results."

Build Supportive Networks: Don't try to navigate these biases alone. Whether through neurodivergent communities, trusted colleagues, or supportive friends, build a network of people who understand your experience and can advocate for you when needed. These allies can help amplify your voice and provide guidance when you encounter resistance.

It's Not About Fitting In—It's About Making the World Fit You

The ultimate goal here is not to mold yourself to fit into neurotypical structures, but to **reshape** your environment so it works for you. Whether you're adapting a workspace, navigating social norms, or pushing back against outdated school policies, remember that you have the power to make adjustments that allow your neurodivergence to thrive.

This doesn't mean the world will always bend to accommodate your needs immediately—but by recognizing the biases in play and advocating for yourself strategically, you can start to carve out spaces where you can be yourself unapologetically. And as more neurodivergent individuals do the same, the world itself will begin to evolve.

The First Steps Toward Understanding: Reflecting on Your Neurodivergence

Embracing your neurodivergence is a journey, and like any journey, it starts with understanding yourself—your strengths, your challenges, and the unique way your brain processes the world. This process of self-reflection is crucial because the more you learn about yourself, the better equipped you'll be to thrive in a society that may not always understand you.

Self-understanding is about more than just identifying your neurotype (though that's an important piece). It's about learning to recognize how your brain functions day-to-day, how it interacts with the world, and how societal structures have shaped your self-image.

What Are Your Biggest Challenges?

Let's start by asking a simple but critical question: **What challenges do you face as a neurodivergent person?**

These challenges could be anything from sensory overload to difficulty with time management, from struggling with traditional communication styles to needing more time to process information. Reflecting on your challenges isn't about seeing them as deficits—it's about gaining clarity on where your pain points are so you can begin addressing them.

Example: "I often feel overwhelmed in loud environments and find it hard to concentrate."

Example: "I struggle with written instructions and need more time to process them."

Once you've identified your main challenges, you'll be better prepared to strategize solutions and advocate for the changes you need.

What Strengths Come Naturally to You?

Just as important as identifying your challenges is recognizing your **natural strengths**. What do you excel at without even trying? What skills or traits make you unique and valuable? These strengths are often the very things that set neurodivergent individuals apart from the neurotypical population.

Example: "I'm really good at spotting patterns that others miss."

Example: "When I'm passionate about something, I can focus intensely and work for hours without getting distracted."

Take some time to reflect on these strengths and think about how they show up in your life. If you're not sure, consider asking trusted friends or colleagues who know you well—they might point out strengths you've overlooked.

How Has Society's Structure Shaped Your View of Yourself?

The way society is structured—from education to workplaces to social expectations—has a huge impact on how you perceive yourself. If you've spent your life feeling out of place or like you were always "doing it wrong," it's time to start questioning whether the problem was ever with you at all.

Reflect on how societal structures may have influenced your self-image:

Were you made to feel "lazy" because of ADHD-related executive dysfunction?

Did traditional schooling leave you feeling "stupid" because dyslexia made reading difficult?

Have you been labeled "rude" or "awkward" for not following social conventions that don't come naturally to you?

These experiences can create internalized self-doubt, but they aren't reflections of your value. Instead, they're reflections of a system that wasn't designed for your neurodivergent brain. The more you unpack these societal influences, the more you'll begin to see how much of your self-perception is tied to external expectations that never served you.

Moving Forward with Empowerment

The process of self-reflection is ongoing, but it's an essential first step toward self-empowerment. As you reflect on your challenges, strengths, and the societal structures that have shaped your view of yourself, you'll begin to unlock a deeper understanding of your neurodivergence—and with that understanding comes power.

The more you learn about yourself, the more confident you'll become in advocating for what you need, pushing back against systems that don't work for you, and creating spaces where you can thrive. And trust me—when you start to see your neurodivergence for what it truly is, you'll realize just how powerful you are.

Conclusion of Chapter 1

With this foundation, you now have a clearer understanding of the landscape of neurodivergence, the strengths and challenges that come with it, and the biases present in neurotypical systems. You've also started the crucial process of self-reflection, which will continue to guide you on this journey.

From here, we'll dive into the heart of the matter—how to **embrace your strengths** and begin flourishing, not in spite of your neurodivergence, but because of it. Your journey toward self-empowerment has just begun, and the road ahead is filled with opportunity.

EMBRACING YOUR STRENGTHS
Chapter 2

Identifying Strengths Based on Your Neurotype

Embracing your strengths begins with understanding that neurodivergence isn't just a challenge—it's a different operating system, one that comes with its own distinct advantages. It's not about waiting for the world to make room for you; it's about carving out that space yourself, starting by recognizing what you bring to the table.

You might have spent a long time feeling like something was wrong with you because you didn't fit into the traditional molds. Maybe you struggled in school, lost focus easily, or found it impossible to follow instructions the way others did. But here's the thing: the problem was never with you. The system wasn't designed with your strengths in mind.

Let me tell you something: **everyone has strengths**—even if it doesn't feel like it. And if you're neurodivergent, your strengths may be exactly what others overlook because they don't recognize their value. The trick is to stop viewing them as quirks or inconveniences and start treating them like superpowers. Trust me, your differences are your biggest asset, but only if you learn to leverage them.

Me-Search

It wasn't until after I was officially diagnosed with Autism that I truly started digging into what makes my brain different. The diagnosis didn't suddenly answer everything, but it opened a door. And once I walked through it, I realized how little I had known about myself.

One of the first times I openly told someone I was autistic, I found myself surrounded by others willing to talk about their own differences. This is where the *real* discovery began. As we exchanged stories, I stumbled across something that blew my mind—literally.

I don't "see" things when I close my eyes. No mental imagery. No pictures. It's not that I don't dream—I do, and my dreams are as vivid as real life. But when I'm awake and try to visualize something, like an apple, there's nothing. Just darkness.

I didn't think much of this until someone else in that conversation casually mentioned how they could picture an apple with full color, details, even a background. I was floored. I started asking around and discovered that this is actually the norm. People can "see" things in their minds. Some can even do it with their eyes open! And here I was, thinking everyone was like me—stuck in darkness when they closed their eyes. Turns out, I have **aphantasia**. And that realization triggered a deep dive into what my brain does differently.

At first, it felt like a huge loss. How could I be missing out on something that others clearly take for granted? But here's the thing: **my brain found ways to compensate.** Sure, I can't visualize an apple, but ask me to imagine an elephant, and I can almost feel where the parts should be. It's like my brain is mapping the object in space without ever showing me the picture. This became especially clear when I realized how much I rely on putting ideas down on paper or into digital form. I'm a designer, and my work involves seeing patterns, trends, and details in ways that others might not. So maybe my brain isn't broken—it just works differently. My inability to produce visuals pushes me to attach to the things I can see in the real world and hyper-focus on them. That's what makes me excel.

But this wasn't just some passive realization. This is what I call *"Me-search"*. It's the years of digging into my brain's quirks and actively turning them into strengths. And no, I'm not talking about some mythical "superpower." I hate that word, honestly. It's overused, and it suggests that neurodivergence automatically makes you some kind of savant. That's not what this is about. This is about taking something that might seem like a flaw and working your ass off to make it an asset.

I started noticing that while I couldn't "see" things, my other senses were more attuned than I'd ever realized. My sense of smell is insane—I can recall smells years later with perfect clarity. In fact, in my first business, I founded a lab that specialized in food and beverage formulation. I helped create thousands of recipes by relying on this heightened olfactory memory. At the time, I didn't understand why I had such a strong sense of smell, but now it's starting to click. It's all connected to how my brain processes information.

Here's the point: **reframing your limitations as strengths** isn't easy. It takes years of self-reflection, hard work, and, frankly, emotional struggle. But it's worth it. This book—and others like it—are tools to help you start that journey. Because no one is going to hand you that understanding on a silver platter. You have to dig for it, just like I did.

I still catch myself saying things like "I can see it now" when I work through ideas, even though I never actually *see* anything. What I'm really doing is conceptualizing. It's like there's a whiteboard in my mind, but instead of visuals, I'm mapping out concepts. That's why I have an unstoppable drive to get those ideas out of my head and into some physical form—whether it's sketching, typing, or designing. It's not about seeing. It's about **building**.

Talking about this has helped me explore it further. I even started using an "apple test" with friends. I'll ask them to close their eyes and picture an apple. Then I'll tell them to move the apple, push it off the table in their mind, and rate how clearly they can see it—from 0 to 5. When I tell them I'm a 0, they're usually shocked. They've never considered that someone might not *see* anything at all. Some people are 10s, others are scattered all over the scale. And every time I find someone who's a 0 like me, it blows their mind that this isn't how everyone's brain works.

I remember being told as a kid to "count sheep" to fall asleep, and all I could think was: **what sheep?** It feels empowering now to know why I could never "see" those damn sheep.

A representation of how people with differing visualization abilities might picture an apple in their mind. The first image is bright and photographic, levels 2 through 4 show increasingly simpler and more faded images, and the last—representing complete aphantasia—shows no image at all

Practical Steps for Identifying Your Strengths

Now that we've talked about recognizing how your brain works differently, let's get down to the practical side of things. This isn't some passive process—you don't just wake up one day knowing your strengths. It takes deliberate effort, reflection, and sometimes even a bit of trial and error. But trust me, the work is worth it because once you figure out what your brain is built to do best, you can start using those strengths to your advantage in every aspect of life.

Here's where to start:

Reflect on Moments of "Flow"

Think back to times when you were completely immersed in something, where time seemed to disappear, and you were fully locked in. Psychologists call this a state of "flow." For many neurodivergent individuals, flow moments happen when we're hyper-focused on something we care deeply about. That's your first clue to identifying a strength.

Maybe you've noticed that when you get deep into a project, you can work for hours without losing focus. Or maybe you have an eye for detail that others miss. These aren't random talents—they're strengths that are often directly linked to how your neurodivergent brain processes information.

Action Step: Take a few minutes to write down three recent moments when you were fully in a state of flow. What were you doing? How did you feel afterward? Identifying these moments helps you see patterns in what activities engage your brain's unique wiring.

Use Strength-Assessment Tools

Sometimes, our strengths are so ingrained in how we think and act that we don't even notice them. That's where tools like the **CliftonStrengths assessment** or the **VIA Character Strengths** survey can help. These tools are designed to highlight the qualities you naturally excel in—things you may overlook because they come so easily to you.

These tests don't ask you to fit into a neurotypical mold; instead, they help you identify the core strengths you can start using in your work, relationships, and personal growth. While these tools weren't designed specifically for neurodivergent individuals, they can still provide valuable insights. You might find, for example, that your natural ability to problem-solve under pressure is one of your greatest assets.

Action Step: Take one of these assessments (many offer free versions online). Once you get your results, compare them to the times you've experienced flow. Where do you see overlap? These are the strengths that will carry you forward.

Journal Your Patterns

Journaling isn't just for introspection—it's a practical way to track patterns in your life. If you want to identify your strengths, you need to see them in action. Start a strengths journal. Each day, jot down one area where you felt competent, energized, or like you contributed something valuable. Don't dismiss the small things—sometimes, your biggest strengths are hiding in the moments you take for granted.

Over time, your journal will become a map of your strengths. You'll notice that certain skills or traits show up repeatedly, and that's where your power lies.

Action Step: Commit to journaling daily for two weeks. At the end of that period, review your entries. What strengths kept coming up? What activities did you feel most engaged in? Your journal will reveal the strengths that might not be obvious at first glance.

Get Feedback from People You Trust

Sometimes, other people see our strengths long before we do. If you're struggling to identify your own, ask for feedback from people who know you well and can give you honest insights. This isn't about fishing for compliments—it's about understanding how your strengths show up in ways you might not recognize.

Action Step: Choose three people in your life who you trust and ask them directly: "What do you think I'm really good at?" The answers might surprise you and give you a new perspective on your natural talents.

Reframe Challenges as Strengths in Disguise

Here's the hard truth: Many of the things that have made life difficult for you are probably linked to your greatest strengths. If you've been told you're too impulsive, too disorganized, or too sensitive, it's time to flip the script. These so-called weaknesses often come with hidden benefits.

For example, impulsivity might mean you're a quick thinker in crisis situations. Being highly sensitive might make you an empathetic leader who can connect deeply with others. These aren't weaknesses—they're strengths in disguise.

Action Step: Write down the challenges or criticisms you've faced because of your neurodivergence. Then, reframe each one as a potential strength. How could that challenge be a hidden asset in the right context?

Taking Action in Spite of Executive Dysfunction

Here's the thing no one tells you: **knowing** what to do and **doing** it are two completely different battles. For a long time, I couldn't understand why I'd read book after book, soaking in all this knowledge about how to improve, how to reach my goals—and then I'd do nothing with it. I wouldn't take a single action step. It's frustrating as hell, because the desire is there. The will is there. But somehow, I'd let it sit until it festered into a problem so big I couldn't ignore it anymore.

That's executive dysfunction at its core. It's not laziness. It's not a lack of desire to improve or a failure to understand what's at stake. It's a disability that makes it hard to bridge the gap between *knowing* and *doing*.

For years, I thought maybe there was something fundamentally wrong with me. I'd see people write notes, set goals, and take action, while I stayed stuck in this endless cycle of *I'll get to it later.* I knew the right steps to take, but they always felt just out of reach. At first, I'd beat myself up over it, thinking, *Am I lazy? Am I just not trying hard enough?*

But here's the truth: **this is the disability portion**. Understanding that my brain is wired this way was the first step to overcoming it. Executive dysfunction doesn't mean you're not capable. It means your brain's wiring makes it harder to start or follow through, even when you want to. The real challenge is finding ways to push through that fog and take action despite it.

 So, how do I do it? I fight for it every single day. Every. Single. Moment.

One of the books that helped me make this shift was *The 10x Rule* by Grant Cardone. I read it about a year ago, and it drilled one thing into my brain: if I want change, if I want to reach my goals, I need to take **massive action**. I'm talking about pushing myself far beyond what feels comfortable, because if I don't, I'll stay exactly where I am. I'll know what needs to be done, but I won't take the steps to do it—and nothing will change.

Here's the part that's hard to admit: I have this false sense sometimes that things will just "work out" on their own, even if I don't make the steps. Like somehow, life will magically fall into place. But I've come to understand that's executive dysfunction talking. It's lying to me. It's the feeling that lets tasks pile up until they explode into a crisis, and then I'll sit there thinking, *How did this happen to me?* But the truth is, **it didn't happen to me—it happened because of me**.

That's a tough pill to swallow, but it's also the key to moving forward. When I'm sitting there, not doing the thing I know I need to do, I have to remind myself: **this won't fix itself.** No one is coming to save me, and everything is **not** going to turn out fine unless I take action.

It's hard. Every time I sit down to write this chapter, or take any step toward a goal, I feel that resistance. My brain wants to wait, to procrastinate, to let it become tomorrow's problem. But I can't let that happen, because the reality is: **if I don't take**

massive action, I'll stay exactly where I am. The only way forward is through.

I remind myself of this constantly—whether I'm working on a book, a business, or just trying to stay on top of daily tasks. And that's what you need to do too. You're not lazy. You're not incapable. You just need to recognize that **executive dysfunction isn't some random problem—it's the thing standing between you and the life you want.** Once you see it for what it is, you can start fighting it. And that's when real change begins.

Action Step: Right now, take 10 minutes to write down one thing you've been putting off—something important. It doesn't matter if it's big or small. Then, commit to taking one small action on it today. The goal isn't to finish it all in one go—it's to get started. Massive action is built on small steps, and those steps are what break the hold executive dysfunction has on you.

Go. Do it. Now. But incase you won't or need help, I will now get more detailed in how to perform these actions steps.

Reframing Challenges as Strengths in Disguise: The Role of Masking

Before we dive deeper into reframing challenges as strengths, there's something we need to address upfront: **masking**. If you're neurodivergent, especially if you're autistic, you've probably been masking for most of your life—whether you realize it or not. Masking is when you suppress your natural behaviors, reactions, or personality traits to fit into neurotypical norms. It's a survival tool, and for many of us, it's second nature.

But masking comes with a cost.

Research shows that masking can lead to significant mental health challenges. Studies have found that autistic individuals who mask often experience higher rates of **anxiety, depression, and burnout**. Why? Because constantly pretending to be someone you're not is exhausting. It disconnects you from your authentic self, making it harder to know where the mask ends and you begin.

So, where does reframing fit into all this? It's simple. A lot of what we've learned to call "masking" is just reframing taken to the extreme. Instead of using it strategically—when it serves a purpose—we use it constantly, often without knowing how to turn it off.

The Double-Edged Sword of Masking

Let's be clear: **masking isn't all bad**. In fact, it can be a necessary tool, especially in environments where being fully yourself could lead to misunderstanding or harm. Think of it like this: when you're in a job interview, you might mask by controlling certain behaviors or emotions to fit the professional setting. That's not inherently negative. In these moments, masking can help you navigate a world that wasn't built for your neurotype.

But here's the key: **masking must be intentional and limited**. When it becomes your default mode—when you're masking 24/7—it starts eroding your sense of self and worsening your mental health. The goal isn't to never mask; the goal is to know **when to mask** and when to let yourself exist as you are, unfiltered.

Reframing Isn't Just Masking with a New Label

Reframing, when done properly, isn't about covering up who you are. It's about recognizing that what the world sees as a challenge—your impulsivity, your sensory sensitivities, your unique communication style—can actually be a strength **in the right context**. It's about using your neurodivergent traits intentionally, rather than suppressing them entirely.

For example, let's say you have a habit of hyper-focusing on one task at the expense of everything else, something that might be viewed as problematic in certain settings. Reframing doesn't mean hiding this behavior—it means recognizing where that hyper-focus could actually be an asset. Maybe you can apply it to a creative project or deep-dive research that requires sustained attention. Reframing is about finding contexts where your traits work for you, not against you.

When to Mask and When to Drop the Mask

So, how do you know when to mask and when to stop? It's a delicate balance that takes time and practice to figure out. The more you understand your strengths, the easier it becomes to navigate this line. Here's where the reframing mindset comes in:

Mask When It's Strategically Necessary: There are times when masking helps you survive and thrive in a world that isn't always designed for you. Job interviews, social situations, and high-stakes environments might require you to mask certain behaviors. The key is to use it *sparingly and intentionally*. Masking for short periods is manageable; it's when masking becomes a permanent state that it starts harming your mental health.

Drop the Mask When You're in Safe Spaces: You need places where you can exist without filtering yourself. Whether it's around close friends, family, or even alone, you must give yourself the space to be fully authentic. Dropping the mask is critical for your mental well-being. This is where you let your so-called "flaws" exist without judgment, and where you start seeing them for what they truly are—parts of you that hold power and potential.

The Mental Health Impact of Chronic Masking

Chronic masking, according to research, leads to **increased mental health struggles**, especially in autistic adults. One study published in the journal *Autism* found that individuals who masked more frequently experienced heightened emotional exhaustion and a greater sense of alienation. Constantly hiding your true self doesn't just drain your energy—it isolates you from the very support systems you need to thrive.

You need to understand that reframing isn't just about finding strength in your neurodivergent traits; it's about learning to balance your need to fit in with your need to be authentic. **Masking all the time is unsustainable**, but strategically applying it can be empowering. The trick is knowing when to turn it off—and that comes with self-awareness.

Action Step: Structuring Your Reflection on Masking and Reframing

Writing down your thoughts might feel overwhelming, especially when you're trying to reflect on something as complex as masking or reframing. Here's how to break it down, step by step. The goal here isn't to write a perfect essay—it's just to get your thoughts out in a way that makes sense to *you*.

Reflect on a Time You Felt the Need to Mask

Think of a recent situation where you felt like you had to mask. Maybe it was a work meeting, a family gathering, or even just running errands. Start by answering these questions:

Where were you? (Be specific: "I was at work, in a meeting with my boss.")

What were you doing? ("I was presenting an idea to my team.")

What did you feel you had to hide or change about yourself? ("I had to suppress my stimming behaviors and keep my voice steady, even though I was anxious.")

Once you've got these down, it'll look something like this:

"Last week, I had to mask during a team meeting at work. I was presenting a project idea, and I felt like I had to hide my stimming behaviors (like tapping my foot) and control my voice so I wouldn't sound anxious. It took a lot of effort to stay 'composed,' and I felt exhausted afterward."

Was Masking Necessary?

Next, ask yourself: *Did I really need to mask in that situation?* Here's how to break that down:

What would've happened if you hadn't masked? ("If I hadn't masked, maybe my boss would've noticed my anxiety, but the meeting would've gone on just the same.")

Did masking help you in that moment, or could you have let your true self show a bit more? ("Masking helped me stay focused on the presentation, but I don't think I needed to suppress my stimming—it might've actually helped me stay calm.")

Your reflection might look like this:

"I think masking helped me stay focused during the presentation, but in hindsight, I probably didn't need to hide my stimming. If I'd let myself stim a little, I might've felt calmer and more grounded."

Create a "Safe Space" List

Lastly, let's identify where you feel safe enough to be yourself without masking. Write down at least three specific places or people where you don't feel the need to suppress your neurodivergent traits:

Environment or people: ("At home with my partner," "When I'm with my close friends," "In my art class.")

Why this space feels safe: ("I don't have to hide my stimming around my partner, and they understand when I need quiet time," "My friends accept me as I am and don't expect me to socialize in a 'normal' way.")

This might look like:

"I feel safe at home with my partner because I don't have to mask around them. They know that I stim when I'm overwhelmed, and they don't pressure me to behave a certain way. Another safe space for me is my art class because it's a quiet, low-pressure environment, and no one expects me to socialize."

By breaking it down this way, you make the process of reflecting less abstract and more structured. The goal is to get something down—no pressure to be perfect or exhaustive, just enough to capture your thoughts in the moment. Remember, this is for *you*, not anyone else. It's about building a habit of checking in with yourself and recognizing where masking fits and where it might not be necessary.

Balancing Masking and Authenticity for Better Mental Health

We've already talked about reframing challenges and how masking is often part of that. But there's another layer to this conversation—learning when masking is necessary and when it's hurting you more than it's helping. Masking, while useful in certain situations, can lead to burnout and mental health challenges when it becomes a permanent way of navigating the world.

If you've been masking for years, it may feel automatic at this point. But **masking 24/7 isn't sustainable**, and that's where the danger lies. **Research** shows that chronic masking is linked to higher levels of **anxiety, depression, and emotional exhaustion**, especially in autistic adults. The constant effort to fit into neurotypical spaces, to filter and hide your true self, takes a toll. That's why learning to balance when to mask and when to let yourself be authentic is crucial for your mental health.

Recognizing When to Mask

Masking, like we said before, is a tool. It's something you can use in certain environments to help you navigate situations that might otherwise be difficult. For example, in a high-stakes meeting, masking can help you get through without drawing unwanted attention. But the key is to use it **strategically**, not constantly.

Mask when it helps you achieve your goals—when it makes life easier or allows you to get through a situation without unnecessary stress. But know when it's time to let the mask drop, too.

When Masking Harms Your Mental Health

The trouble comes when masking becomes constant, even in safe environments. You might start feeling like you can't relax, even around people who care about you. Or you might forget what it feels like to be yourself without filtering everything. That's when masking crosses the line from being a helpful tool to becoming harmful.

The result? Burnout, emotional exhaustion, and a sense of isolation—even when you're surrounded by others. This constant suppression of who you are is exhausting, and it chips away at your mental health over time. It's not something you notice right away, but eventually, you hit a wall.

So, how do you find the balance? How do you use masking in a way that serves you without letting it take over your life?

Action Step: Learning When to Mask and When to Be Authentic

Let's take a structured approach to figure out where masking serves you and where it might be hurting you. Here's how to break it down, step by step:

Identify Situations Where You Feel You Have to Mask

Start by listing three specific situations where you feel the need to mask your neurodivergent traits. These could be work-related, social situations, or even family gatherings. Write down:

Where were you? ("At a family dinner.")

What did you feel you had to hide or change? ("I had to force myself to keep eye contact and suppress my need to stim.")

Why did you feel you had to mask? ("I didn't want to make my relatives uncomfortable or draw attention to myself.")

Your reflection might look like this:

"At a family dinner, I felt like I had to mask by keeping eye contact and suppressing my stimming because I didn't want to make my relatives uncomfortable or seem out of place."

Consider the Cost of Masking

Reflect on how masking in those situations made you feel. Did masking help you achieve your goal, or did it leave you feeling exhausted, disconnected, or anxious afterward? Ask yourself:

Did masking help you achieve something? ("Yes, I got through the dinner without anyone commenting on my behavior.")

Did masking leave you feeling drained or disconnected? ("Yes, I felt completely exhausted afterward and needed time alone to recover.")

This might look like:

"Masking helped me get through the dinner without drawing attention to myself, but afterward, I was so drained that I had to go home and isolate for the rest of the night."

Identify Where You Can Be Authentic

Now, think about where you feel safe enough to drop the mask. These are your "authentic" spaces—environments where you don't feel the need to filter your behavior or pretend to be someone else.

Where do you feel safe to be yourself? ("When I'm at home alone," "With my best friend.")

What behaviors do you feel comfortable expressing? ("I can stim, like tapping my fingers, or avoid small talk without feeling judged.")

Your response might look like:

"At home with my best friend, I can stim freely, like tapping my fingers or avoiding eye contact, and they don't judge me. I feel safe being myself."

Set Boundaries for When to Mask and When to Let It Go

Finally, it's time to set some boundaries for yourself. Choose one situation where you can start dropping the mask more often, even if it's just in small ways. Then, identify situations where masking is still necessary but can be limited.

Where can you start being more authentic? ("At work, I'll allow myself to stim discreetly during meetings, like tapping my leg, without feeling ashamed.")

When do you still need to mask? ("In client presentations, I'll continue to mask certain traits like my lack of eye contact, but I'll stop masking my need to take notes to stay focused.")

Your response might look like this:

"At work, I'll allow myself to stim discreetly during meetings by tapping my leg under the table, instead of forcing myself to sit completely still. But in

high-pressure presentations, I'll keep masking my lack of eye contact for now while letting myself take notes openly to stay engaged."

By figuring out when to mask and when to be yourself, you're protecting your mental health and setting boundaries that will help you thrive. Remember, masking is a tool—it's something you can choose to use strategically, but it should never be something that defines you.

How to Take Control of Your Narrative

By now, we've talked about recognizing your strengths, reframing challenges, and balancing when to mask and when to be authentic. But here's the most important part of all: taking control of your own narrative. It's about deciding how you want to show up in the world—not letting anyone else tell you who to be or how to think.

For years, you've probably had people define you based on your neurodivergence. Maybe they've labeled you as too much—too sensitive, too intense, too distracted. Or maybe they've labeled you as not enough—like you're not trying hard enough, or you're not capable of "normal" things. Those labels get heavy after a while, and if you're not careful, they start to shape your identity.

But you're not here to live inside someone else's narrative. You're here to write your own story—one that's built on your strengths, not your limitations.

The only way to take back control is to recognize the power of your own voice. You're the only person who truly knows what's happening in your mind, and you're the only one who can decide how to navigate the world with the brain you've got. This isn't about conforming to someone else's expectations. It's about showing up fully as yourself, on your terms.

Shifting from Survival to Ownership

Many of us have spent most of our lives in **survival mode**—just trying to get through each day without being noticed, judged, or misunderstood. Masking is a big part of that survival instinct. But survival isn't enough anymore. You need to move from **survival** to **ownership**. It's not just about making it through the day; it's about deciding how you want to live and thrive, not just fit in.

Reframing the Way You See Yourself

Start by recognizing that your neurodivergence isn't something to hide or manage—it's something to **own**. The more you try to suppress who you are, the harder it becomes to live authentically. You can't grow into your full potential when you're constantly apologizing for how your brain works. Stop apologizing. Instead, start acknowledging the value that comes from being different.

Let's reframe the way you see yourself, your struggles, and your strengths:

You're not "too sensitive"—you're deeply in tune with emotions, both yours and others'. That's empathy, and it's a skill that makes you a better friend, partner, and leader.

You're not "impulsive"—you're decisive and able to act quickly when others get stuck in overthinking.

You're not "distracted"—you're naturally curious and able to jump between different ideas, often discovering connections that others miss.

This isn't about sugarcoating reality or ignoring your challenges. It's about recognizing that your neurodivergence comes with strengths that the world often overlooks. And it's up to you to bring those strengths to the surface.

Owning Your Story Publicly

There's power in sharing your story. Owning your neurodivergence publicly isn't about broadcasting it to everyone, but about choosing when, where, and how to share it in a way that benefits you and those around you. This might mean telling your boss that certain accommodations help you work better, or opening up to a friend about why you struggle in loud social environments.

By sharing your story, you're helping to break down the stigma that surrounds neurodivergence. You're showing people that being different isn't a flaw—it's a different way of thinking that can drive innovation, creativity, and empathy. When you tell your story, you take ownership of it. It's no longer something that happens *to* you—it's something you're in control of.

Action Step: Crafting Your Narrative

Let's start small by crafting the narrative you want to share with the world. You don't have to dive into a full-on autobiography here. Instead, focus on a few key areas that define how you want to be seen and how you want to see yourself.

Define Three Key Traits that Make You Unique

Start by identifying three traits that you want people to know about you—traits that make you uniquely *you*. These don't have to be "positive" or "perfect" traits—they just need to be authentic. Write them down:

Trait #1: ("I'm deeply empathetic.")

Trait #2: ("I'm curious and always learning.")

Trait #3: ("I'm creative and think outside the box.")

Your response might look like:

"I want people to know that I'm deeply empathetic. I'm always curious and constantly learning new things, and my creativity helps me think outside the box when solving problems."

Write a Short Statement About Your Neurodivergence

Next, write a simple statement about how your neurodivergence shapes who you are. You're not looking to create a whole speech here—just a sentence or two that expresses how your brain works differently and how that makes you stronger.

Example: "Being autistic means I think in patterns and systems, and it helps me approach problems in a unique way that others might not see."

Your response might look like this:

"As someone with ADHD, my mind works fast, which means I can connect ideas quickly and find creative solutions in high-pressure situations."

Share Your Story When It Matters

Lastly, think about where and when you might share your story. This doesn't mean telling everyone you meet about your neurodivergence. It means identifying situations where sharing your story will benefit you and help others understand you better.

Where might you share your story? ("I might share my story with my boss so they understand why I work better with flexible deadlines.")

Why is it important to share here? ("By sharing, I'll be able to advocate for myself and get the accommodations I need to thrive.")

Your response might look like this:

"I'll share my story with my boss to help them understand why I need flexible deadlines and

quiet workspaces. This will allow me to be more productive and reduce the stress of masking at work."

By taking control of your narrative, you're not just surviving—you're owning your neurodivergence in a way that empowers you. This isn't about seeking approval or validation from others. It's about embracing the fact that your brain works differently, and that difference is what makes you exceptional.

IT'S TIME TO RISE.
Chapter 3

The Birth of the RISE Framework

If you had met me as a teenager, you would have seen someone who didn't have a shot. Homeless for a time, sleeping in abandoned apartments, begging for change just to eat—it was a fight for survival, day by day. I didn't want the luxury of thinking about the future. Back then, the idea of starting a business, much less one that would get acquired and eventually grow to $50 million in annual revenue, wasn't even in my vocabulary. But here's the thing: when I realized the world didn't expect me to survive, let alone thrive then that's exactly why I had to.

Fast forward through years of grinding, learning, and failing forward, and I eventually built a business that was acquired by a publicly traded company. I went on to create my own consulting and creative agency, working as an executive producer for celebrities and Fortune 500 brands. But what people don't see on the outside is the daily struggle of living with autism and other neurodivergent traits. It's not easy, and it never will be. No matter how much success I've achieved or failures I stumble into, I wake up every day facing the same challenges. The difference is that I've developed a way to push through them.

That's where the **RISE Framework** comes in.

I didn't come up with RISE sitting in a university classroom, studying neurodiversity with a Ph.D. or a stack of psychology textbooks. In fact, I don't have a formal degree or any academic credentials to my name. What I do have is lived experience—years of trial and error, fighting through personal struggles, and learning how to not just survive but thrive as a neurodivergent individual.

RISE started with me. It's what I use to turn my struggles into strengths every single day. It's not a theory; it's a practical methodology that I live by. I've spent years developing this framework, refining it, and applying it in my personal and professional life. It's how I've managed to build a life that

I'm proud of despite my disabilities. I choose to reframe my challenges every hour, every moment, into opportunities.

Working with the **Southwest Autism Research and Resource Center (SARRC)**, as a founding member of their self-advocate advisory board, has been one of the most rewarding experiences of my life. I've had the privilege of working with other autistic adults—some, like me, who have the ability to reframe their challenges, and others who will never be able to advocate for themselves. Some can't even speak. That reality keeps me grounded. No matter how hard my days get, I remind myself that it could always be worse. At least I have the ability to choose—to take action, to push forward, to reframe my disabilities into strengths.

The RISE Framework isn't just a tool; it's a mindset, one that helps me function at a high level in my work, with clients, and in everyday life. It's the reason I can manage the pressure of working with celebrities, Fortune 500 brands, and multi-million-dollar deals. Without this internal methodology, I wouldn't be able to handle it.

My goal with RISE is simple: I want to help others like me. People who struggle with the same challenges, who need a structure to rely on when things get overwhelming. RISE helped me, and I believe it can help you too. Whether you're at the beginning of your journey or trying to manage life at a higher level, this framework can be the foundation that keeps you grounded, focused, and ready to embrace your neurodivergence as a strength.

Every time I need to get started, I say "It's time to RISE"

Now that we've laid the foundation with my personal journey and the origins of the RISE Framework, it's time to dive into what this framework truly means and how it can help you embrace your neurodivergent strengths.

The **RISE Framework** is more than just a set of steps; it's a mindset. It's how I've navigated my life—from facing overwhelming challenges to achieving success on my own terms. RISE stands for:

- **R: Recognize** – Recognize and understand the unique strengths and challenges associated with neurodiversity. This includes acknowledging different ways of thinking and processing information.

- **I: Inspire** – Inspire yourself and others to embrace their neurodiverse traits and utilize them as strengths. Encouragement to pursue personal and professional goals with confidence.

- **S: Support** – Provide support and strategies for managing challenges related to neurodiversity. This includes techniques for improving communication, organization, and self-advocacy.

- **E: Empower** – Empower individuals to take control of their lives and careers by leveraging their unique abilities. This involves fostering a sense of self-worth and the confidence to succeed in various environments.

This framework has helped me, not just to survive, but to thrive in environments that were never built for people like us—it's how I am going to reach a goal of changing the world for us—it's my new mantra. It's allowed me to function at a high level while working with multi-million-dollar clients and leading projects with celebrities and Fortune 500 brands—all while managing my own neurodivergent challenges. But more importantly, it's helped me **accept myself** as I am, without constantly fighting to be something I'm not.

RISE isn't about perfection. It's about progression. Each step is designed to move you closer to fully embracing who you are, using your unique strengths to get there. You're not here to fit into a mold. You're here to create your own path.

But First, It's About Me.

Before I can help anyone else, before I can teach this framework to others, I have to admit something: RISE wasn't created for everyone at first. It was built out of my own personal need to survive, thrive, and function in a world that wasn't designed for people like me. It's selfish in the best way possible.

I had to take care of myself first. I had to find a system that helped me manage my day-to-day challenges, that pushed me to embrace my strengths, and that allowed me to turn my so-called weaknesses into opportunities for growth. Only after I had this framework in place for myself could I then expand it to help others.

In a sense, **RISE** started as a tool to help me navigate my own neurodivergent mind. It was about finding a way to succeed in my life—on my terms—before I could begin teaching others to do the same. And this is where I want to challenge you: before you can help anyone else, before you can use your neurodivergence as a tool for success in relationships, work, or advocacy, you need to **start with yourself.**

This framework only works if you use it for you first. You have to **recognize** your own traits, **inspire** yourself to action, **support** your own growth, and **empower** yourself to take control of your life.

RISE for Me: Focusing on ME in Each Step

Now that we've discussed how the RISE Framework is structured, let's break down each step into how it applies **specifically to you**—and how you can apply it to yourself as an individual. Each part of RISE starts with "Me, Myself, and I". This isn't about what others can do for you. It's about what *you* can do for yourself, starting with self-care and self-awareness.

The next part is what I created for myself. It may not apply to you, but it will help you start to craft your own steps.

R: Recognize

Recognizing my own strengths and challenges has been the foundation for everything. I had to understand how my brain worked before I could leverage it. I'm not just talking about the big, obvious things. It's the little details that make a huge difference. I had to learn to recognize how I process information differently, how my sensory sensitivities affect me, and how my unique thinking patterns shape my approach to problem-solving. Without this, I would never have been able to reframe these traits into something valuable.

How to use it:

- I recognize that I struggle with sensory overload, so I take proactive steps to manage it, whether that means creating a quieter workspace or using noise-canceling headphones during intense periods.

- I also recognize that I thrive in high-focus situations, so I set up my environment in a way that encourages deep work, breaking tasks down into chunks where I can hyper-focus without distraction.

I: Inspire

I have to inspire myself every single day. No one else is going to do it for me. It's easy to get bogged down by challenges, by the feeling that I don't fit in, or by the constant pressure to mask and adapt.

But I've learned that the only way to push through is to **inspire myself** to keep going. This isn't about blind optimism—it's about **real** encouragement. It's about reminding myself that my neurodivergent traits are my strengths, not my weaknesses.

How I use it:

- Every day, I make a point to focus on one thing I've accomplished, no matter how small. This reinforces my belief that I'm capable of achieving my goals, even when things feel overwhelming.

- I also set visual reminders in my workspace—quotes, achievements, or milestones—to inspire me when I'm facing self-doubt or moments of exhaustion.

S: Support

Before I can support others, I have to support myself. That means putting systems in place that work for *me*, not for how neurotypicals expect me to function. I had to learn how to manage my executive dysfunction, improve communication in my relationships, and develop tools for staying organized. This is about setting up the right support network, tools, and strategies to make life manageable—so I don't crash and burn.

How I use it:

- I rely on tools like apps and digital planners to manage my daily tasks, breaking things down so I'm not overwhelmed by too many projects at once.

- I also lean on a core group of people—mentors, friends, and family—who understand my neurodivergence and provide the emotional support I need when things get tough.

E: Empower (For Me)

Empowerment is about owning my neurodivergence and using it to my advantage. I had to stop waiting for others to tell me it was okay to be different. I had to own it. Empowerment for me meant taking control of my life—my business, my relationships, my daily routines—by leveraging the unique abilities that come with being neurodivergent.

How I use it:

- I empower myself by setting realistic but ambitious goals, knowing that I can use my creative problem-solving skills to achieve them.

- I remind myself daily that I have the ability to **take action**—even when I'm feeling overwhelmed by executive dysfunction or other challenges. Empowerment means taking those small, uncomfortable steps to keep moving forward.

The Takeaway: RISE Begins With You

The **RISE Framework** isn't just about helping others—it's about helping *yourself* first. It's about building a foundation of self-awareness, self-care, and self-empowerment before you can share your strengths with the world. I had to learn this the hard way: if you don't take care of yourself, you'll never have the energy or the tools to help others.

Start by applying RISE to your own life. Recognize your strengths, inspire yourself, build the support systems you need, and empower yourself to live fully. Only then can you use this framework to support others in their own journeys.

Defining RISE for Yourself

Now that you've seen how I use the RISE Framework in my own life, it's time for you to define what RISE means for you. Each letter of the framework—**Recognize, Inspire, Support, Empower**—is a stepping stone toward self-acceptance and growth. But to make it work, you need to personalize it. This isn't about following a rigid formula—it's about crafting a system that fits your unique neurodivergence and life circumstances.

Use the following steps to define **RISE** in a way that works specifically for you.

R: Recognize – Understanding Your Unique Strengths and Challenges

Recognition is the first step toward self-acceptance. To embrace your neurodivergence, you need to understand how your brain works. What are the strengths and challenges that come with your neurodivergent traits? Recognizing these is crucial because it allows you to lean into your strengths while finding ways to manage or reframe your challenges.

Action Step: Define "Recognize" for Yourself

Take a moment to reflect on the traits that define your neurodivergence. Use the prompts below to help you recognize both your strengths and challenges:

- **What strengths come from your neurodivergence?**

    ◦ Example: "I can focus deeply on tasks that interest me, allowing me to achieve a level of detail others often miss."

- **What challenges do you face because of your neurodivergence?**

    ◦ Example: "I struggle with sensory overload in noisy environments, which can make it difficult to concentrate."

Your Reflection:

Write down at least two strengths and two challenges you've recognized in yourself. How do these shape your daily life? How have they influenced your personal and professional journey?

- **Strength #1:**

- **Strength #2:**

- Challenge #1:

- Challenge #2:

I: Inspire – Encouraging Yourself to Embrace Your Neurodivergence

Inspiration is about shifting your mindset. It's not enough to just recognize your traits—you need to **inspire yourself to use them** as strengths. This means embracing your neurodivergence and using it as a tool to pursue your personal and professional goals with confidence. The inspiration has to come from within—you have to remind yourself that your unique way of thinking is valuable.

Action Step: Define "Inspire" for Yourself

Think about how you can use your strengths to inspire yourself to take action. Consider the following prompts:

- **What goal or dream have you been hesitant to pursue?**
    - Example: "I've always wanted to start my own business but have held back because I wasn't sure if I could handle the challenges."
- **Which neurodivergent strength can help you achieve that goal?**
    - Example: "My creativity and ability to see the big picture will help me develop a business that stands out."

Your Reflection:

Write down one goal you want to achieve and link it to a strength that will help you reach it. Then, write a small action you can take this week to get closer to that goal.

- **Goal**:

- **Neurodivergent Strength:**

- **Action for This Week:**

S: Support – Building Systems and Strategies for Success

Support is about recognizing that you can't do everything on your own—and that's okay. You need tools, strategies, and people who can help you manage your challenges and grow. This includes using organizational tools, self-care routines, or leaning on supportive friends and professionals who understand your needs.

Action Step: Define "Support" for Yourself

Think about the systems and support networks you need to thrive. Use the prompts below to help you identify what works for you:

- **What tools or resources help you manage your challenges?**
    - Example: "I use a digital planner to organize my tasks and manage my time, breaking big projects into smaller, more manageable steps."
- **Who in your life provides emotional or practical support?**
    - Example: "My best friend understands my neurodivergence and is a sounding board when I feel overwhelmed."

Your Reflection:

Write down one tool or resource that supports your growth, and one person who helps you emotionally or practically. Then, think about how you can lean into these supports more effectively.

- **Tool/Resource**:

- **Support Person:**

E: Empower – Taking Control of Your Life and Career

Empowerment is about taking ownership of your neurodivergence and using it to your advantage. It's about believing in your unique abilities and having the confidence to succeed in environments that weren't designed for people like you. Empowerment is where you stop trying to fit in and start creating spaces that work for you.

Action Step: Define "Empower" for Yourself

Consider what empowerment looks like in your life. How can you start taking control of your personal and professional life by leveraging your neurodivergent traits? Use these prompts to guide you:

- **Where in your life would you like to feel**

more empowered?

- Example: "I want to feel more empowered in my career, especially when it comes to advocating for accommodations that will help me thrive."

- **What neurodivergent trait can you leverage to take control?**

  - Example: "I'm great at thinking outside the box, which helps me develop creative solutions to work-related problems."

Your Reflection:

Write down one area where you want to feel more empowered and how you can use your strengths to take control in that space. Then, list one action you can take this month to step into that empowerment.

- **Empowerment Area:**

- **Strength to Leverage:**

- **Action for This Month:**

Taking RISE Personally

By defining each part of the RISE Framework for yourself, you're starting to take control of your neurodivergent journey. Remember, **this is about you first.** You need to recognize your strengths and challenges, inspire yourself to act, build support systems that work for you, and empower yourself to succeed in environments that weren't built with you in mind.

RISE isn't about changing who you are—it's about **owning who you are** and using that to your advantage. Now that you've defined RISE for yourself, revisit this framework often. As you grow, your understanding of these steps will evolve, and that's exactly how it should be.

Continuing the Journey: RISE Never Ends

The process of applying the **RISE Framework** isn't something you do once and forget about. It's an ongoing practice. You'll find that your strengths evolve, your challenges shift, and your goals grow over time. As you move forward, remember that RISE is here to guide you through every phase of your life, and it's okay to revisit these steps as often as you need to.

There will be days when you feel completely aligned with your strengths and empowered by your neurodivergence. And there will be days when the challenges feel overwhelming. That's normal. The key is to keep coming back to the framework. **Recognize** where you are today, **Inspire** yourself to take one intentional step forward, **Support** yourself with the right tools and people, and **Empower** yourself to keep progressing—even if it's one small, focused step at a time.

You are on a journey of self-acceptance and growth, and it's one that you control. **RISE** is your tool to navigate this path—not perfectly, but purposefully. You don't have to rush it. You don't have to get it all right the first time. Just remember to keep moving forward. **RISE never ends—it's the foundation for your lifelong journey.**

Your Personal RISE Action Plan

Before closing this chapter, take a moment to commit to your next steps. What's the one area of your life where you want to focus the most right now? Whether it's recognizing a new strength, finding better support, or empowering yourself in a challenging situation, write it down. Make a plan for the next month, and commit to revisiting it regularly.

- **Focus Area for This Month:**

- **Action Step:**

- **How Will You Measure Your Progress?:**

You don't need to take huge leaps all at once—just one focused action at a time. This is your journey, and every effort you make toward self-acceptance, growth, and empowerment matters. Remember, **it's time to RISE**—and you're the one in control of that journey

NAVIGATING THE NEUROTYPICAL WORLD

Chapter 4

The Reality of the Neurotypical World

Living as a neurodivergent individual in a world designed for neurotypicals can feel like trying to navigate an environment where the rules are never fully explained. The systems, social norms, and unspoken expectations of society are built around the way neurotypical minds operate, often leaving neurodiverse individuals feeling out of sync, misunderstood, or even alienated. The reality is that most of the environments we encounter—workplaces, schools, social settings—are structured to accommodate neurotypical behaviors, and this can create significant challenges for neurodivergent people.

It's important to acknowledge that this isn't a level playing field. The neurotypical world isn't necessarily hostile to neurodivergent people, but it operates on assumptions that may not account for different ways of thinking, feeling, or processing information. Many of these assumptions are subtle, and they often go unnoticed by neurotypical individuals because they are so ingrained in the way they interact with the world.

Setting the Stage: Most Environments Are Designed Around Neurotypical Behaviors

When we talk about environments being "designed for neurotypicals," we're referring to both the **physical** and **social structures** that make up our daily lives:

Physical environments: Think of the typical workplace or classroom. They are often set up in ways that prioritize multitasking, constant stimulation, and group interaction, which can be overwhelming or even impossible for neurodivergent people. Open-plan offices, for instance, assume that workers can focus amidst noise and movement. For someone with sensory sensitivities or attention issues, this setup can be debilitating.

Social environments: Neurotypical social expectations include behaviors like **small talk**, **maintaining eye contact**, and **reading between the lines**. These norms are so deeply ingrained that neurotypical people don't even realize they're following them—but for neurodivergent people, understanding and conforming to these social rules can feel like trying to decode a hidden language.

The world expects neurodivergent individuals to adapt, to fit into these structures, often without offering any flexibility or accommodations. This reality can be exhausting. It can feel like you're constantly bending to fit into an uncomfortable mold.

But here's the thing: **you don't have to conform to these expectations**. The goal isn't to erase your neurodivergence or try to blend in at all costs. The goal is to **navigate these spaces effectively**, understanding the rules well enough to play by them when necessary, but also knowing when to push back or ask for changes that accommodate your needs.

Navigating vs. Conforming

Many neurodivergent people spend their lives **masking**—hiding their neurodivergent traits in order to appear "normal." This can be physically and emotionally draining, leading to burnout, anxiety, and depression. The world pushes us to conform because neurotypical behaviors are considered the standard, but constant conformity comes at a cost.

The alternative is **learning to navigate** the neurotypical world without losing yourself in the process. The goal is not to conform to neurotypical standards for the sake of fitting in, but to understand the behaviors and expectations well enough that you can **choose** when to adapt and when to stay authentic to your neurodivergent self.

Let's break that down:

Conforming means erasing or masking your true self to fit into neurotypical norms. It might involve forcing eye contact even though it makes you uncomfortable, pretending to enjoy small talk, or suppressing stimming behaviors that help you manage anxiety or sensory overload.

Navigating, on the other hand, means understanding the social codes, behaviors, and expectations of neurotypical people so that you can participate when it's necessary, but without compromising your mental health or well-being. It's about having the knowledge and the tools to say, "I understand what's expected here, and I'll engage in a way that works for me."

For example, in a work meeting, you might know that eye contact is expected to show engagement, but instead of forcing prolonged eye contact, you can **strategically glance up** from time to time or make eye contact when speaking, balancing their expectations with your comfort.

In social settings, you can recognize that small talk is part of the "social glue" that holds conversations together. While it may feel pointless, engaging in it for a few minutes can help establish rapport before you steer the conversation toward something more meaningful or comfortable for you.

Navigating means choosing when to adapt and when to remain authentic—knowing when to "play the game" and when to advocate for your needs or simply be yourself.

A Lifelong Learning Process: The Reality of Trial and Error

Here's the hard truth: learning to navigate the neurotypical world is a **lifelong process**. There's no guidebook that will teach you every social rule or expectation. The landscape of neurotypical behavior is complex, and it varies across cultures, professions, relationships, and even generations.

For neurodivergent individuals, the challenge is often **trial and error**. You might find yourself in situations where you feel misunderstood or out of place, not because you're doing something wrong, but because the unspoken rules of neurotypical behavior are difficult to predict or decode.

For example:

- You might think you're having a direct conversation, only to realize later that the other person was hinting at something completely different.

- You might struggle to understand why people get upset when you interrupt them to share an exciting thought, not realizing that neurotypical social norms discourage interruptions, even when the intention is positive.

Learning these things often involves **making mistakes**, but that's part of the process. Each interaction, each experience in a neurotypical environment, teaches you more about how these unspoken rules work—and how to navigate them in ways that are **strategic** without compromising who you are.

As a neurodivergent person, you will constantly be learning the nuances of neurotypical behavior, and that's okay. The point isn't to become perfect at playing their game—it's to get better at understanding it, so you can **decide when and how to engage**.

By understanding that most environments are designed for neurotypical people and learning to navigate those spaces without feeling forced to conform, you can begin to build a roadmap for thriving. It's not about following every neurotypical social rule, but about learning enough to interact effectively, protect your mental health, and choose when to adapt or advocate for changes.

In the sections that follow, we'll dive deeper into the specific social norms, expectations, and unspoken rules of the neurotypical world—and explore how you can navigate them in a way that works for you, without losing yourself in the process.

Understanding Neurotypical Social Norms

Navigating neurotypical spaces as a neurodivergent person can feel like playing a game where the rules are constantly changing, or worse, never fully explained. Neurotypical individuals often follow invisible social scripts and expect others to pick up on them naturally. These expectations may feel unnecessary, arbitrary, or even confusing for people with autism, ADHD, dyslexia, dyspraxia, or other neurotypes. But learning to understand these unwritten rules can help neurodivergent individuals interact more effectively, avoid misunderstandings, and reduce the social friction they may face.

Let's explore **common neurotypical social norms** that neurodivergent individuals might struggle with, alongside strategies for managing these situations.

The Importance of Social Cues

Neurotypical communication relies heavily on **social cues**—those non-verbal signals and behaviors that convey meaning without directly stating it. For neurodivergent people, especially those with autism or ADHD, these cues can be difficult to interpret, leaving you feeling confused or out of sync with the conversation.

Here's a breakdown of some of the most common social cues neurotypical people use, and what they often mean:

- **Body Posture**: Neurotypical people often use body language to communicate engagement or disinterest. Leaning forward signals interest, while leaning back or crossing arms may suggest discomfort or disinterest. For someone with autism, this might not register as a cue at all, which could lead to unintentional misunderstandings.

- **Example**: If a colleague leans forward during a conversation, they may be signaling that they're engaged and interested in what you're saying. If they start leaning back or looking at their watch, it could be a cue that they're ready to end the conversation. Picking up on these signals helps you know when to wrap up or change the topic.

- **Facial Expressions**: Neurotypical people expect facial expressions to match the conversation. A neutral or blank expression might be misinterpreted as indifference.

Neurotypical people also expect smiling, nodding, or other expressions to show empathy or agreement.

- **Example**: When someone shares personal news, a lack of a smile, nod, or concerned facial expression could be read as indifference, even if that's not how you feel. For those with ADHD or autism, who may have a different relationship with facial expressions, this can be confusing. In certain situations, practicing small gestures—like a simple nod or brief smile—can go a long way in signaling empathy.

- **Proximity and Personal Space**: Neurotypical people have fairly strict unspoken rules about personal space. Standing too close can feel invasive; standing too far away might make them feel disconnected. However, personal space rules can vary by culture, gender, and the relationship you have with the person.

- **Example**: In professional settings,

neurotypical individuals typically stand about an arm's length away during conversation. In more intimate settings (like with close friends), standing closer is acceptable. But if you're unsure, observing how others behave and maintaining the same distance is a helpful guideline.

The "How Are You?" Dilemma

One of the most basic neurotypical social conventions is the question: **"How are you?" or "You Alright?"**. For neurotypical people, this is usually just a polite way to say hello—it's not really a request for detailed information. However, for neurodivergent individuals, especially those on the autism spectrum, this can be confusing. It seems like a straightforward question, so why not answer it honestly?

Here's the catch: **"How are you?"** is typically a surface-level pleasantry in neurotypical culture. It's often just a way to initiate conversation or acknowledge the other person, with the expectation that the response will be equally brief, like **"I'm good, thanks"** or **"Doing well, and you?"**, or "**Yeah You?**" if in UK. With all of the other parts of the world, I'm sure I'm leaving out a few.

- **Example**: If you respond to **"How are you?"** with a detailed answer—like explaining how your day is actually going or what's bothering you—neurotypical people might feel uncomfortable or even confused. They weren't expecting that level of openness.

- **What You Can Do**: You can still be honest without going into too much detail. If you don't feel like answering **"I'm good"**, try saying something like **"Not bad, hanging in there"** or **"Doing okay, thanks for asking"**. These answers satisfy the social expectation without requiring you to mask your feelings entirely.

Small Talk as Social Glue

For neurotypical individuals, **small talk** is a way to build rapport. It's not about exchanging deep or meaningful information; instead, it's about creating a connection through short, pleasant exchanges. Topics like the weather, weekend plans, or general observations are common in small talk, and while this might seem trivial or pointless to neurodivergent people, it serves as a bonding ritual for neurotypicals.

- **Example**: When a co-worker asks **"Did you do anything fun this weekend?"**, they likely aren't expecting a detailed itinerary of your weekend activities. Instead, they're making a friendly gesture to show they're interested in connecting on a social level. Responding with a simple **"Oh, nothing too exciting. Just relaxed a bit, and you?"** keeps the conversation light and fulfills the expectation.

- **What You Can Do**: If small talk feels unnatural, view it as a **stepping stone** toward more meaningful conversations. Think of it as a tool, not a distraction. You can engage in it briefly to build rapport, then shift to a topic you find more engaging or important. If you feel overwhelmed, have a few standard responses prepared, like **"Same old, same old"** or **"Nothing much, how about you?"**

Politeness and the Avoidance of Directness

Another common neurotypical social norm is the tendency to prioritize **politeness** over directness. Neurotypicals often avoid saying things that might be perceived as too blunt or confrontational, even when the situation calls for clear communication. For neurodivergent individuals, especially those with autism or ADHD, this can lead to confusion because the indirectness seems inefficient or even dishonest.

- **Example**: Instead of saying, **"I don't like this idea,"** a neurotypical person might say, **"That's an interesting perspective"** or **"I'm not sure that would work right now."** They're essentially rejecting the idea, but they avoid saying it outright to avoid hurting your feelings.

- **What You Can Do**: Recognizing this tendency can help you interpret neurotypical conversations. When you hear vague or neutral language, it might be a polite way of signaling disagreement or discomfort. You can ask for more specifics if needed, saying something like, **"Do you have any concerns about this idea?"** or **"Can you tell me what you think might not work?"**

Tone and Volume of Voice

Neurotypical people are often sensitive to the **tone** and **volume** of voice during conversations. Speaking too loudly can be interpreted as aggressive, while speaking too softly might signal a lack of confidence. The tone of your voice—whether it's perceived as friendly, neutral, or irritated—also communicates emotional context, sometimes even more than the words you use.

For neurodivergent individuals, especially those with **sensory processing issues** or **ADHD**, managing tone and volume can be challenging. You may not realize your voice has gotten louder due to excitement or frustration, or you might speak in a flat tone when you're feeling tired, which others could interpret as disinterest.

- **Example**: In a meeting, if your voice rises in volume while you're passionately explaining an idea, a neurotypical person might assume you're getting upset or confrontational, even if you're just enthusiastic.

- **What You Can Do**: Being mindful of how tone and volume are perceived in neurotypical environments can help smooth over communication. Practice modulating your voice during conversations, or ask trusted colleagues or friends for feedback on how your tone is coming across. You might also preface a conversation by saying something like, **"I'm excited about this idea, so I might sound more intense than I mean to"** to give context for your tone.

The Expectation of Formal Greetings and Farewells

Neurotypical social norms include formalities around **greetings** and **farewells** that might feel repetitive or unnecessary to neurodivergent individuals. In professional settings, greetings like **"Good morning"** or **"Hello"** are expected when starting the day or entering a room, even if no immediate conversation follows. Similarly, **saying goodbye** before leaving a group or a meeting is seen as a necessary formality.

For neurodivergent individuals, especially those who feel drained by social interaction or those who don't see the point in unnecessary pleasantries, this can seem like an arbitrary ritual. However, to neurotypicals, skipping these greetings or farewells can come across as abrupt, dismissive, or even rude.

- **Example:** Walking into the office and going straight to your desk without greeting anyone may lead neurotypical colleagues to assume you're upset or unfriendly, even if you're just focused on your work or feeling socially tired.

- **What You Can Do**: If formal greetings feel draining, keep them brief but consistent. A simple **"Hey"** or **"Good morning"** when entering a room can help you fit into the social flow without committing to a full conversation. Similarly, saying **"Take care"** or **"Have a good one"** when leaving a meeting satisfies the expectation without requiring too much effort.

Navigating Invitations and Declining Social Events

Another common neurotypical norm is the expectation around **invitations** to social events and how to **politely decline** them. Neurotypical people often extend invitations as part of a social ritual, even if they don't expect every person to attend. For neurodivergent individuals, especially those with social anxiety or those who find group events overwhelming, this can create internal conflict: you may not want to go, but you don't want to offend anyone by declining.

- **Example**: A co-worker invites you to a casual happy hour after work. You're exhausted from the day and don't feel up to socializing, but you worry that saying no might seem rude or distant.

- **What You Can Do**: Neurotypical people often don't take it personally if you decline an invitation, as long as you do so politely. Saying something like, **"I appreciate the invite, but I'm going to sit this one out. Maybe next time!"** or **"Thanks for thinking of me, but I have something else planned"** is a socially acceptable way to decline without feeling guilty or pressured.

It's also worth noting that in some cases, declining an invitation repeatedly might lead neurotypical people to assume you're not interested in socializing at all. If you do want to maintain connections but can't always attend events, occasionally suggesting alternatives, like meeting for coffee or lunch one-on-one, can keep the relationship going on terms that are more comfortable for you.

The Silent Expectation of Reciprocity in Conversations

In neurotypical conversations, there's often an unspoken expectation of **reciprocity**—if someone shares something personal or asks you a question, they usually expect you to reciprocate by sharing something similar or asking a related question in return. Neurodivergent individuals may not always pick up on this expectation, especially if the conversation feels like it should naturally move on to a different topic.

- **Example**: A colleague shares details about their weekend, and after they finish, they expect you to do the same. If you respond with a simple **"That's nice"** or shift the topic, it might feel to them like you're not engaged or willing to share.

- **What You Can Do**: To navigate this, you

can try mirroring the conversational pattern. If someone shares something personal, you don't have to give a detailed response, but offering something in return helps the conversation flow in a way that feels natural to neurotypicals. You might say, **"That sounds fun! I spent my weekend catching up on some reading"** or **"I had a pretty quiet weekend myself, thanks for asking."** This keeps the exchange balanced and fulfills the expectation of reciprocity.

Eye Contact Expectations

One of the most common and challenging social norms for neurodivergent individuals, particularly those with autism or ADHD, is the expectation around **eye contact**. In neurotypical culture, making eye contact is often associated with engagement, respect, and attentiveness. Conversely, avoiding eye contact can be interpreted as disinterest, nervousness, or even dishonesty. These assumptions are deeply ingrained in many cultures, and neurotypicals may not even realize that they're making these judgments based on something as simple as eye contact.

For neurodivergent individuals, maintaining eye contact can be a **sensory challenge** or simply not a priority in how they process information. For some, particularly those with **autism**, maintaining direct eye contact can feel intrusive or even painful, while for others, it can be an overwhelming distraction from the conversation itself. Those with **ADHD** might find their attention pulled in different directions, making it hard to focus on maintaining eye contact when they are busy processing the verbal content of the conversation.

Why Eye Contact is Important in Neurotypical Culture

In neurotypical communication, eye contact is considered an essential part of non-verbal communication. It often signals:

- **Engagement and interest**: Maintaining eye

contact shows the speaker that you are paying attention and interested in what they are saying.

- **Trustworthiness**: Eye contact is often interpreted as a sign of honesty and transparency. Avoiding eye contact might make someone seem evasive or dishonest, even if that's far from the truth.

- **Confidence**: In professional settings, particularly, eye contact is often seen as a sign of confidence and assertiveness. Someone who avoids eye contact may be perceived as uncertain or timid, regardless of their actual competence.

For neurotypicals, eye contact flows naturally as part of conversation. They may not be aware that maintaining it could be uncomfortable or even physically distressing for someone who processes sensory input differently. This expectation can create significant misunderstandings or lead to judgment, especially in professional settings or first impressions.

Challenges for Neurodivergent Individuals

For neurodivergent individuals, especially those on the autism spectrum, eye contact can pose several challenges:

- **Sensory Overload**: Maintaining eye contact can feel like too much input. Looking directly at someone's eyes can cause sensory overwhelm, making it harder to process the actual conversation. It can also trigger anxiety for those with **social anxiety** or **autism**, as it may feel invasive or too intimate.

- **Distracting from the Conversation**: Many neurodivergent individuals, particularly those with **ADHD,** find that eye contact diverts their focus from the conversation. When trying to maintain eye contact, their brain might struggle to concentrate on the content of the discussion because they are also expending energy on maintaining this social expectation.

- **Difficulty in Reading Social Cues**: For some neurodivergent people, especially those with **autism**, maintaining eye contact while also trying to read facial expressions and other social cues can be overwhelming. It's difficult to simultaneously process all the visual information and the verbal content of the conversation, leading to discomfort and disengagement.

- **Cultural Expectations**: For neurotypicals, avoiding eye contact might be interpreted as being disengaged, disrespectful, or even dishonest, regardless of the neurodivergent individual's actual behavior or intent. This is particularly problematic in professional settings like job interviews, where eye contact is often judged as a sign of confidence and competence.

Strategies for Navigating Eye Contact Expectations

It's important to strike a balance between understanding neurotypical expectations around eye contact and managing your own comfort levels. You don't have to force yourself into uncomfortable or overwhelming situations, but there are ways to navigate these expectations while still honoring your needs.

- **Brief Glances**: Instead of maintaining direct eye contact throughout the entire conversation, try using brief glances. Look at the person when you are speaking or listening to something important, then look away naturally. You don't have to lock eyes the entire time to show engagement; short bursts of eye contact can be enough to meet neurotypical expectations.

- **Alternative Focus Points**: If direct eye contact feels too intense, you can focus on the person's forehead, nose, or even a point just over their shoulder. This creates the illusion of eye contact without causing the sensory overwhelm that comes from directly looking into someone's eyes.

- **Set Expectations When Possible**: In more familiar or supportive environments, it's okay to explain your preference for less eye contact. You might say something like, **"I focus better when I'm not maintaining eye contact, but I'm fully engaged in what you're saying."** This not only sets expectations but also helps educate others about neurodivergent needs.

- **Practice in Low-Stakes Environments**: If you want to become more comfortable with eye contact in situations where it might be important (like job interviews or public speaking), practicing in low-stakes environments with people you trust can help. This way, you can develop a strategy that works for you without the pressure of a high-stakes interaction.

- **Acknowledge When It's Difficult**: In certain professional or social situations where eye contact is heavily emphasized (such as interviews), you can briefly acknowledge that it's difficult for you.

You might say, **"I sometimes have trouble maintaining eye contact, but it doesn't mean I'm not engaged or confident in what I'm saying."** This allows you to manage expectations without masking your needs.

When It's Okay to Skip Eye Contact

In many settings, especially with friends, family, or understanding colleagues, it's okay to forgo eye contact altogether. Authentic communication matters more than conforming to every neurotypical social norm, especially if that norm is causing you distress or discomfort. If eye contact is draining, you can prioritize managing your own well-being by engaging in the conversation in other ways—through your words, tone, or gestures.

You don't have to force yourself into behaviors that feel unnatural or uncomfortable to you in order to fit in. The goal is to **navigate** neurotypical spaces in a way that respects their norms while maintaining your own boundaries and comfort levels.

Eye contact is one of the most deeply ingrained social expectations in neurotypical culture, and while it may come naturally to neurotypical individuals, it can be a significant challenge for neurodivergent people. By understanding the reasons behind the expectation and using strategies to manage it, you can navigate situations where eye contact is expected while protecting your own comfort and mental well-being.

Remember, you don't have to maintain perfect eye contact to be a good communicator. Balancing neurotypical expectations with your personal boundaries is the key to thriving in social and professional settings.

Conclusion: Understanding Neurotypical Norms

Navigating the world of neurotypical social norms can feel like an ongoing challenge, and the examples we've covered—social cues, small talk, eye contact, turn-taking, indirect communication, and more—are just the tip of the iceberg. The reality is, we could fill an entire book exploring the vast range of unspoken rules and expectations that neurotypicals follow without even realizing it. For neurodivergent individuals, understanding these norms isn't just about fitting in—it's about learning how to interact in ways that feel manageable and authentic.

But this process is never finished. There will always be new social situations, new environments, and new nuances to learn. And that's okay. The key isn't to master every norm or adopt every behavior—it's to continue growing your understanding, so you can make informed decisions about when to adapt and when to advocate for your needs. Over time, with awareness and practice, you'll be able to navigate neurotypical spaces more confidently while staying true to who you are.

Ask Yourself: What Neurotypical Norms Have You Noticed?

As you reflect on what we've covered, take a moment to think about your own experiences. Have you encountered other neurotypical norms that didn't make sense to you at first? Are there social rules you've had to learn over time? Recognizing these patterns is a powerful step in understanding how to engage with them on your own terms.

Here are a few prompts to get you thinking:

- Have you noticed any unspoken rules in your workplace, social circles, or family that you've had to figure out?

- Are there situations where neurotypical expectations have made you feel misunderstood or out of place?

- How have you navigated these moments, and what strategies have worked for you?

Encouragement to Keep Learning

The learning process doesn't stop here. Every interaction is a chance to expand your understanding of how neurotypical norms work and, more importantly, how you can navigate them in a way that protects your mental health and well-being. The more you observe, the more you'll notice patterns—and the more equipped you'll be to decide when to adapt and when to embrace your authentic neurodivergent self.

Continue to grow by:

- **Paying attention** to social interactions in your daily life and reflecting on how neurotypical people behave.

- **Asking questions** or seeking clarification when you're unsure about social expectations. Most people will be happy to explain if they realize you're genuinely trying to engage.

- **Finding balance** between understanding these norms and not feeling pressured to conform to them all the time. Remember, you have the right to set boundaries and prioritize your own comfort.

It's not about changing who you are—it's about gaining the tools to navigate a world that wasn't designed with neurodivergent people in mind. With continued learning and self-awareness, you'll be able to grow into your full potential, using these insights to help you thrive in both neurotypical and neurodivergent spaces.

Communication Norms in Neurotypical Environments

When it comes to communication, neurotypical individuals often follow a set of unspoken rules that can be puzzling to neurodivergent people. Neurotypical communication frequently prioritizes **politeness** and **indirectness** over precision, which may feel counterintuitive if you're used to being direct, especially if you have autism, ADHD, or a similar neurodivergent profile. These nuances can make communication tricky, especially if you're someone who values clarity and tends to approach conversations in a straightforward manner.

In this section, we'll dive deeper into three critical aspects of neurotypical communication: the preference for **politeness over precision**, the art of **reading between the lines**, and the **timing of interruptions**—a social minefield for many neurodivergent individuals. Understanding these norms can help you navigate neurotypical spaces with more confidence while maintaining your authenticity.

Politeness Over Precision

In many neurotypical environments, particularly in professional or social settings, **politeness** often takes precedence over **precision**. This means that neurotypical people may avoid directly expressing their thoughts or feelings, opting instead for softer, more roundabout language to maintain social harmony and avoid discomfort. This can be confusing for neurodivergent people, especially those who value directness and clarity, like many individuals with autism or ADHD.

Understanding the Role of Politeness

Neurotypicals often prioritize social cohesion over direct communication. In their view, being too blunt can be seen as rude or confrontational, even if the information is necessary or the intention is positive. As a result, they may speak in **euphemisms** or **understate** their true feelings in order to soften the impact of their words.

For neurodivergent individuals, this can feel frustrating, especially if you're someone who values clear, unambiguous language. You might find yourself wondering why people don't just say what they mean.

- **Example**: Imagine a work situation where a colleague says, **"That's an interesting approach"** or **"I can see where you're coming from."** These might sound like neutral or even positive comments, but in a neurotypical context, they could be polite ways of disagreeing or signaling that they're not fully on board with your idea.

Why Neurodivergent Individuals Struggle With This Norm

For many neurodivergent people, especially those on the autism spectrum, communication is valued for its **functional** and **informational** quality. You might be more comfortable saying exactly what you think or feel, with the belief that the clearest, most accurate language is the best way to get the point across.

But in neurotypical environments, being too direct can sometimes backfire. Neurotypical people might misinterpret directness as **aggression** or **insensitivity**, leading to unintended social friction. This creates a dilemma for neurodivergent individuals who want to be honest but also don't want to alienate others.

Navigating Politeness Without Losing Precision

Here are a few strategies for navigating this delicate balance:

- **Mirror Neurotypical Language**: In situations where you feel the need to be polite but still want to maintain precision, consider **mirroring** the softer language that neurotypical people use. For example, if someone says, **"That's an interesting perspective,"** and you disagree, you could respond with something like, **"I can see how you'd feel that way, though I'm leaning toward a different approach."** This allows you to voice your opinion without coming across as too blunt.

- **Pre-Frame Your Directness**: If you need to be direct, especially in professional settings, you can **pre-frame** your comments by acknowledging the difference in communication style. For example, **"I tend to be straightforward in my communication, so please know that I'm coming from a place of respect when I say this."** This signals to the listener that your intention is not to offend but to communicate clearly.

Reading Between the Lines

Many neurotypical conversations involve **implied meaning**. Instead of saying what they mean outright, neurotypical individuals often expect others to **read between the lines**, picking up on subtle hints or indirect language. For neurodivergent people, particularly those with autism, this expectation can feel like navigating a minefield of unspoken social rules.

The Nature of Implied Meaning

Neurotypical people frequently communicate in ways that **suggest** rather than **state**. This indirect style allows them to maintain politeness and avoid confrontation, but it can be incredibly frustrating if you're someone who prefers clarity.

- **Example**: A co-worker might say, **"It's getting late, isn't it?"** as a way of hinting that they're ready to end a meeting. Instead of directly saying, **"Let's wrap up,"** they rely on you to infer the real meaning behind their words.

For someone who processes language literally, like many people with autism, it's easy to miss these implied meanings. You might take the statement at face value—yes, it is getting late—without realizing they're signaling that the conversation should end.

Why Neurodivergent Individuals Struggle With This Norm

Many neurodivergent people, particularly those on the autism spectrum, tend to **process language more literally**. If something isn't explicitly stated, it might not register as part of the conversation. This can lead to situations where neurotypical people think they've communicated something clearly, while you're left feeling confused or unsure of what they really meant.

For example, someone might say, **"I'm fine,"** but their body language or tone suggests they're upset.

If you're not tuned into those non-verbal cues, you might miss that they're implying the opposite of what they're saying.

How to Read Between the Lines

While it may not feel natural, learning to listen for **context clues** can help you better interpret what's really being said:

- **Look for Patterns in Tone or Body Language**: Often, neurotypical people will pair indirect language with certain non-verbal cues, like sighing, crossing their arms, or using a more irritated tone of voice. By paying attention to these cues, you can start to pick up on the **implied emotions** behind the words.

- **Clarify When in Doubt**: If you're unsure about the meaning behind someone's words, it's perfectly okay to ask for clarification. You might say, **"Just to make sure I'm understanding correctly, are you saying**

we should end the meeting now?" This helps avoid misunderstandings and shows that you're engaged in the conversation.

The Timing of Interruptions

In neurotypical culture, conversations are expected to follow a **turn-taking** structure, where each person speaks in turn and interruptions are typically seen as rude. Neurotypical social norms prioritize **waiting for a pause** in the conversation before jumping in, even if what you have to say feels important. For neurodivergent individuals, particularly those with ADHD or autism, this can be a significant challenge because you may naturally want to **jump in when a thought occurs**—either because you're excited, worried you'll forget what you want to say, or because you're not picking up on the subtle signals that it's someone else's turn to talk. This is one of my personal struggles I work to improve every day yet still have not mastered.

Why Timing Interruptions is Difficult

For neurodivergent individuals, the **timing of interruptions** often feels less about social rules and more about the flow of thought:

- **ADHD**: If you have ADHD, your thoughts might race, and when you have something to contribute, it feels urgent to say it before the thought slips away. Neurotypical people may interpret this as being impatient or rude, when in reality, you're simply trying to keep up with your own mind's rapid pace.

- **Autism**: For someone with autism, you might not pick up on the non-verbal signals that it's someone else's turn to speak. Neurotypical people might use subtle body language—like leaning back, gesturing, or pausing briefly—to indicate they're about to continue talking, but without explicitly stating it. If these cues aren't obvious to you, you might jump in prematurely.

Why Interruptions are Frowned Upon

For neurotypicals, conversation is often viewed as a **cooperative exchange**, with each person expected to wait their turn. Interrupting, even with a valid point, is seen as breaking the social contract, leading to the perception that you're **not listening** or **don't respect** the other person's time to speak. This can cause frustration and misunderstandings, even if your intention is purely excitement or engagement.

Strategies for Managing Interruptions

If waiting your turn in conversation feels unnatural, here are some strategies that can help:

- **Mentally Note Key Points**: If you have a point you're eager to share but it's not your turn, try **mentally noting** or writing down the key idea. This allows you to hold onto your thought without feeling the need to interrupt. You can then bring it up once there's a natural pause in the conversation.

- **Look for Pausing Cues**: Neurotypical people often use subtle signals to show when they're done speaking, such as pausing, making eye contact, or gesturing toward you. Learning to recognize these cues can help you gauge when it's your turn to jump in.

- **Politely Ask to Jump In**: If you feel like you're bursting to say something and can't wait, it's okay to ask permission to briefly interrupt. You might say something like, **"Sorry to interrupt, but I just wanted to add something quickly before I forget."** This shows respect for the other person's turn while acknowledging your need to contribute.

Neurotypical communication is full of subtleties and unspoken rules that can be difficult for neurodivergent individuals to navigate. Whether it's the emphasis on **politeness over precision**, the need to **read between the lines**, or the challenge of **timing interruptions**, these norms often feel confusing or counterintuitive.

But by understanding these expectations and learning to interpret the hidden cues in neurotypical conversations, you can develop strategies that help you communicate more effectively without losing your authenticity. Remember, you don't have to completely change how you communicate—rather, you can **enhance your social toolkit** by learning when and how to adapt in ways that feel manageable for you.

Neurotypical Expectations in Professional Settings

Navigating the workplace as a neurodivergent individual is often a delicate balance between authenticity and adaptation. While the world is gradually becoming more aware of neurodiversity, the reality is that most professional environments are still structured around neurotypical behaviors and expectations. These workplaces often expect employees to conform to traditional work habits—like multitasking, participating in small talk, and following formal communication styles—that may feel unnatural or even counterproductive for neurodivergent individuals.

For many neurodivergent people, masking—the act of suppressing or hiding neurodivergent traits to fit in—is a common survival tool in professional settings. But masking comes at a cost, often leading to exhaustion, burnout, and a loss of self-identity. At the same time, neurodivergent employees face the challenge of knowing when to push for accommodations and when to adapt, recognizing that while the law may support workplace accommodations, the real-world application of these rights is often inconsistent.

In this section, we'll explore how to navigate these expectations, with a focus on balancing authenticity, masking, and self-reflection to maintain mental well-being while building a successful career. We'll also consider how tools like AI and platforms like ChatGPT can assist in adapting to these environments—something that could eventually become part of the RISE Framework itself.

"Fitting In" at Work: The Pressure to Conform to Neurotypical Behaviors

In most workplaces, there is a subtle but significant expectation to fit in by adopting neurotypical work habits. For neurodivergent individuals, especially those with autism, ADHD, or dyslexia, these expectations can feel exhausting, and the pressure to conform often leads to masking—the act of hiding your true self to fit societal norms.

Neurotypical Work Behaviors and Their Impact:

- **Multitasking**: In many jobs, multitasking is considered a valuable skill. Employees are expected to juggle multiple tasks simultaneously and switch between different projects on a whim. For someone with ADHD or autism, multitasking can feel chaotic and counterproductive. Hyperfocus, a strength for many neurodivergent individuals, allows you to dive deeply into one task, but this often goes unrecognized in work environments that prioritize fast, scattered attention.

- **Socializing During Breaks**: Office culture often values social engagement—whether it's chatting by the coffee machine, joining colleagues for lunch, or participating in team-building activities. Neurotypical people see these interactions as ways to build relationships, but for neurodivergent individuals, especially those with autism or social anxiety, these moments can feel draining and unnecessary. Forcing yourself to engage in small talk just to fit in can lead to prolonged masking, which adds to emotional exhaustion.

- **Conforming to Rigid Workflows**: Workplaces often enforce specific ways of organizing tasks, setting priorities, and maintaining productivity. For neurodivergent people, especially those with dyslexia, dyspraxia, or executive dysfunction, these rigid workflows might not align with your natural way of processing information. You may have unique organizational methods that work well for you but aren't easily accepted by neurotypical peers or supervisors.

The Reality of Masking at Work

Masking in the workplace often feels like the only way to survive and keep up with neurotypical expectations. However, the cost of constantly masking can't be ignored. Neurodivergent individuals frequently experience:

- **Burnout**: The emotional and mental exhaustion that comes from pretending to be something you're not in order to avoid standing out or facing criticism.

- **Identity Erosion**: Over time, masking can cause you to lose touch with your authentic self. When you spend so much time adjusting your behavior to meet external expectations, it becomes harder to maintain a sense of self.

- **Stress and Anxiety**: Constantly monitoring your behavior, language, and interactions creates an underlying stress that can contribute to anxiety, particularly in high-stakes professional environments.

Strategies for Navigating "Fitting In" While Staying True to Yourself:

- **Selective Masking**: Recognize when masking is necessary for survival in certain professional environments and when it's worth advocating for your own needs. It's okay to mask in situations where you feel it's needed, but avoid doing it all the time. Learn to selectively mask when necessary but prioritize moments where you can be your authentic self, especially during breaks or when interacting with trusted colleagues.

- **Advocate for Your Strengths**: Rather than focusing on multitasking, emphasize your ability to hyperfocus and complete deep work with accuracy and efficiency. For example, you might say, "I find that I work best when I can dedicate focused time to one task at a time, and I'll deliver high-quality results this way."

- **Balance Social Interaction**: If socializing during breaks feels overwhelming, find ways to balance social interaction with self-care.

Use break times to recharge in quieter spaces or set boundaries around how much you engage in office small talk. Over time, you'll identify which interactions are worth your energy and which ones you can avoid without negative repercussions.

Emails and Tone: Navigating Neurotypical Expectations in Written Communication

Professional communication, particularly through email, presents its own set of neurotypical expectations that can feel confusing or frustrating to neurodivergent individuals. Email tone, in particular, is a minefield, with neurotypicals often relying on a balance of formality and indirect language that prioritizes politeness over precision. For neurodivergent people, especially those who prefer clarity and directness, this can lead to misunderstandings or the fear of appearing blunt or rude.

The Challenges of Email Communication:

- **Indirect Language**: Neurotypicals frequently soften their requests or feedback in written communication. Instead of saying, "I need this by the end of the day," they might write, "It would be great if you could have this finished by the end of the day, if possible." This vague phrasing can cause confusion, leaving you unsure about the real urgency of the task.

- **Overly Formal Tone**: Many workplaces expect emails to have a professional tone, often filled with pleasantries and indirect requests. Phrases like, "I hope this email finds you well," or "I'm just following up to see if you had a chance to look at..." are common. While these are considered polite by neurotypical standards, for neurodivergent individuals who prefer getting straight to the point, this can feel cumbersome and unnecessary.

- **Fear of Misinterpretation**: If you tend to write emails in a more direct and concise manner, neurotypical colleagues might perceive your tone as cold or blunt. What you see as efficient communication could be interpreted as unfriendly or even rude by those who expect more social padding.

Using AI Tools and ChatGPT to Help with Emails

One potential solution is to leverage AI tools like ChatGPT, Claude or whatever AI tool is easiest for you to help craft emails that meet neurotypical expectations without requiring you to overthink every response. By inputting your straightforward email into AI, you can generate a more polished version that includes the expected pleasantries or softens the tone without losing clarity. I have even created a custom GPT that knows my tone and personality and maintains it while modifying the output for neurotypical reading––it's a lifesaver!

Example: You could write, "I need this by tomorrow," and ChatGPT might adjust it to, "Just a friendly reminder that we'll need this by tomorrow. Thanks for your attention to this!" This approach allows you to focus on the message while AI handles the softer nuances.

A Future Tool for RISE?: As I continue developing tools for neurodivergent individuals, perhaps a future version of the RISE Framework could include AI-driven tools that assist with professional communication. A tool that helps neurodivergent individuals translate their direct communication into neurotypical-friendly formats could help reduce workplace stress and miscommunication.

Strategies for Navigating Email Expectations:

- **Use Templates**: Create a set of email templates for common scenarios that include the expected polite language, so you don't have to reinvent the wheel each time. For example, a follow-up email template might start with, "I hope this message finds you well," and end with, "Thank you for your attention to this matter." This allows you to maintain professionalism without overthinking.

- **Ask for Clarification**: When you receive an email with indirect language, it's okay to ask for clarification. If you're unsure about the urgency or expectation behind a vaguely worded request, you could respond with, "Just to confirm, do you need this by the end of the day, or is there flexibility with the deadline?"

- **Be Transparent About Your Communication Style**: If you feel comfortable, let colleagues know that you tend to be more direct in your emails but are always happy to clarify tone or intention. You might say, "I like to keep my communication efficient, but please feel free to let me know if my tone ever comes across as too blunt. It's never my intention."

Managing Sensory Overload in the Workplace

Workplaces are rarely designed with sensory sensitivities in mind, and this can be particularly challenging for neurodivergent employees, especially those with autism, ADHD, or sensory processing disorder. The constant noise, bright lights, and interruptions in modern offices—especially open-plan environments—can lead to sensory overload, making it difficult to concentrate, stay productive, or even

The Hard Truth

I've spent my entire life trying to find a place that would accept me—somewhere I could show up as my authentic self without having to hide or apologize for being different. And, after years of searching, I've realized that for people like us, that place might not exist in the traditional sense. For me, becoming an entrepreneur was the only way I could create a space where I could truly be myself. Running my own business gave me the freedom to set my own rules, to build an environment where my neurodivergence wasn't just accepted—it was an asset.

But let's be clear: entrepreneurship has its own set of challenges, and that journey comes with ups and downs, which I'll save for another day. The point is that for many neurodivergent individuals, the idea of fitting into a typical 9-to-5 structure might never feel right. You might find yourself bouncing from one job to the next, constantly feeling like you're forcing yourself to mold into something that's just not you. It's exhausting.

The truth is, there's no one-size-fits-all solution. You'll likely struggle. You'll learn, and then you'll struggle some more. And just when you think you've figured it out, you'll find that the journey isn't over—it never really is. For some of you, the process of trial and error will eventually lead you to a workplace that feels like a good fit, a space where your strengths are recognized and your differences are respected. But for many of you, that perfect environment may never come. And that's okay. It's not a reflection of your worth or your ability.

The peace you're seeking, that sense of truly belonging, might not be something that exists out there in the world. It might be something you have to cultivate within yourself. This doesn't mean giving up on finding a good job or a supportive team, but it does mean taking ownership of your journey. The more you understand yourself—your strengths, your needs, your limits—the more control you'll have over how you navigate these environments.

You may not find the perfect workplace, but you can create the balance you need to thrive. That balance comes from building resilience, learning how to advocate for yourself, and giving yourself grace during the hard days. This journey isn't easy, and it's not quick. But in taking the time to grow, reflect, and adjust, you'll eventually find a way to operate in the world on your own terms, without losing who you are in the process. And that is a kind of peace—one that comes from within, rather than relying on the external validation of finding the "right" place.

Sometimes, that inner peace comes from knowing that you don't need to fit in. Instead, you can carve out your own path, even if that means challenging the very systems that seem to push you out. And in doing so, you'll discover that the only place you really need to belong is within yourself.

Understanding Neurotypical Body Language and Non-Verbal Communication

Here's the thing: you might already be picking up on way more body language than you realize. The tricky part? It's all happening beneath the surface. You catch a quick twitch in someone's face, a shift in their posture, or a sudden change in their tone, and suddenly, you're left wondering, *Is this about me?* You're not wrong in sensing something—but here's the catch: it might not have anything to do with you.

Micro-expressions: Your Hidden Superpower

Let's start with micro-expressions. These tiny, lightning-fast facial cues that flash across someone's face before they can even think about controlling them. It's like the truth sneaking out for a second before being tucked away again. Neurotypical people might miss them entirely, but we often don't. The wild part? We pick them up so fast that sometimes, we don't even consciously know we're doing it. You're reading the emotional room quicker than you think, but because it's happening so subtly, you might not fully understand what you're picking up or why.

Here's the thing though: just because you sense frustration, anger, or confusion doesn't mean it's about you. Someone might frown while they're replaying a fight they had earlier or wince at a memory—and you're left standing there thinking, *What did I just say?* It's easy to get caught up in this emotional whirlwind, assuming that every flicker of discomfort is a response to you. Spoiler alert: it's usually not.

That's the tricky part for neurodivergent folks like us. We're often hyperaware, soaking up every little shift in expression, but we don't always know what to do with that information. It's like having a super-sensitive radar that's always on, but no one gave us the instruction manual. The key is learning to pause and separate your observations from assumptions. Just because you saw something doesn't mean it's *about* something you did.

Facial Expressions and Gestures: Not Just About the Words

Neurotypicals are masters of non-verbal communication. They speak with their hands, their faces, their posture—sometimes more than with actual words. A raised eyebrow could mean they're skeptical. A half-smile might be polite, but not genuine. And while they're playing this game of unspoken meaning, we're left trying to figure out which signals are real and which ones are just background noise.

For many of us, this feels like trying to decode a language we never learned. You see the smile but can't tell if it's a friendly "I like you" smile or an "I'm pretending to be nice" one. And the worst part? We might not naturally use those same signals ourselves. People might think we're disengaged or distant because we don't mirror their expressions or gestures. But you know what? That doesn't mean you're disconnected. It just means you're wired differently.

The challenge here is that neurotypicals expect you to *get* this language without ever teaching it. And while that's frustrating, there's power in knowing you don't have to play along in the same way. You can start to observe these patterns and decide what to do with them on your own terms. Sometimes, just being aware of this can give you a clearer path forward, especially in work or social situations.

Personal Space: The Unwritten Rulebook

Ah, personal space. Neurotypicals seem to have this invisible map of how much space is "right" in any given situation. Too close? You're creepy. Too far? You're distant. And these rules shift depending on the relationship, the setting, and even the mood of the moment. For a lot of us, this map feels fuzzy at best, confusing at worst.

The key here is to understand that personal space isn't just physical—it's emotional. How close someone stands to you, how they lean in or pull back, often signals trust or hesitation. Neurotypicals navigate this naturally, while we might not even realize there *is* a map. Here's what helps: start with a little more space than you think is necessary, especially with new people or in unfamiliar environments. Then, watch how they adjust. Do they lean in? Step closer? That's your cue to do the same.

On the flip side, if someone's too close for your comfort, it's okay to create a bit of distance. Neurotypicals often respond to these subtle shifts without even realizing it. You're allowed to make the space you need, both physically and emotionally.

Tone and Volume: When Words Are Only Half the Message

Here's where things get especially dicey—tone and volume. How you say something can completely change its meaning in a neurotypical world. Speak softly, and you might come off as insecure or unsure. Speak loudly, and suddenly you're "too intense" or "aggressive." It's like walking a tightrope where the volume dial is constantly shifting.

For us, this can be a major source of confusion. You might feel like your tone is neutral, but others hear frustration or irritation. Or maybe you're passionate about something, and it's misinterpreted as anger. Neurotypicals read tone and volume like a map—they expect you to hit the right note every time. If you don't, they jump to conclusions about your mood or intent.

But here's something to remember: you're probably just as sensitive to tone as they are, if not more. You notice the tiniest shift in someone's voice, and suddenly the entire mood of the conversation feels different. Sometimes, you might be reacting to a change that no one else even noticed. It's like having finely tuned speakers that pick up every crackle and whisper in the audio. Knowing this about yourself can help you pause, check in with the context, and decide whether that shift in tone is actually significant—or just part of the noise.

The Struggle with Masking and the Cost of Adapting

Let's talk about masking. It's one of those survival mechanisms that most neurodivergent people develop early, often without even realizing we're doing it. You slip into a version of yourself that feels *acceptable* to others, and before you know it, you're spending more time performing than living authentically. Masking might help you navigate the world smoothly on the surface, but underneath? It's exhausting. It drains you, leaves you questioning who you really are, and worse, it often feels like you're losing yourself in the process.

What is Masking?

Masking is like putting on a costume, but instead of it being for Halloween or a party, it's an everyday thing—something you wear to fit in, blend in, and avoid standing out too much. It's the way we suppress or hide traits that don't align with neurotypical expectations. Maybe it's forcing eye contact when it feels uncomfortable, or holding back from talking about your special interests because they might seem too intense for others. Masking can be faking small talk at work when all you want is to skip the pleasantries, or mimicking facial expressions to seem more "approachable" even when you're feeling overwhelmed inside.

It's a tool—one that many neurodivergent people develop to survive in a world that wasn't built for them. But here's the thing: masking isn't just about conforming to social norms, it's about protecting ourselves. We mask because we've learned, through subtle cues and outright rejection, that who we naturally are might not be accepted. So we adjust, adapt, and shrink ourselves down to fit into spaces that don't always feel welcoming. In doing so, we often hope to avoid misunderstanding, rejection, or judgment.

But what if I told you that while masking helps us navigate the world, it comes with a price—one that's often invisible until we hit a breaking point?

The Emotional Toll of Masking

The toll of masking can be immense, and it's not always immediate. Think of masking like running a marathon in a heavy suit of armor. At first, you can manage—it feels doable, and maybe even necessary. But over time, that armor weighs you down, drains your energy, and leaves you utterly exhausted.

The emotional cost of constantly masking is real. One of the biggest impacts? *Burnout.* When you spend so much energy suppressing who you are to meet the expectations of others, you start to deplete your emotional reserves. You get tired, not just physically, but mentally and emotionally. It's the kind of tired that sleep doesn't fix, because it's deeper than just a lack of rest—it's a fatigue that comes from denying yourself, day after day.

And then there's the *identity confusion.* After a while, it can get hard to tell where the mask ends and where you begin. Who are you, really? Are you the person who performs at work, or the person who decompresses at home, finally letting the mask slip away? The longer you mask, the blurrier that line becomes. It's like constantly switching between characters in a play, and eventually, you forget which role is the real you. That's a terrifying feeling, the sense that you're losing touch with your true self, buried beneath layers of adaptation.

Another major consequence is the *emotional disconnection* that masking can create. When you're constantly presenting a version of yourself that isn't quite real, it can feel like the people around you aren't connecting with the true you. They're interacting with your mask, not with you. That can be incredibly isolating, even in a room full of people. It creates a sense of loneliness that's hard to shake because no matter how much you're surrounded by others, you're not being *seen.* Not really.

Let's not forget the *anxiety* that often accompanies masking. You're constantly on high alert, watching yourself, second-guessing your actions, trying to predict how others will react. It's like being stuck in performance mode all the time, wondering if you'll be found out or if your mask will slip at the wrong moment. And this anxiety feeds into *self-doubt,* making you question whether you'll ever be enough just as you are, without the mask.

Knowing When to Mask and When to Be Authentic

This is the tricky part—finding that balance between masking when you need to and giving yourself permission to show up authentically. Let's be real: we live in a world where masking can sometimes feel necessary, especially in certain environments. There are situations where it's a survival tool, where adapting to neurotypical expectations helps you get through the day, keep your job, or avoid conflict. But here's the thing: you don't have to wear the mask *all* the time. In fact, you shouldn't.

So, how do you know when to mask and when to let your true self come through? It starts with *recognizing the cost* of masking in different situations. If you find yourself constantly masking at work, for example, take note of how it's affecting you. Do you feel drained at the end of the day? Do you dread interactions because they require so much effort to maintain the mask? If the cost of masking is consistently leading to burnout or emotional exhaustion, it might be time to evaluate how much you're adapting versus how much you're sacrificing.

One key is learning to *strategically mask*—to use it when absolutely necessary, but to allow your authentic self to shine through in environments that feel safer. Maybe that means masking during a stressful meeting at work but being fully yourself with friends or family who accept you. Or perhaps it's finding moments throughout the day where you can let down your guard, even briefly, to recharge. The goal isn't to abandon masking altogether—it can be a useful tool—but to use it more sparingly, in ways that protect your well-being.

Another piece of this puzzle is learning how to create spaces where you *don't* have to mask. Whether that's finding a supportive group of friends, a neurodivergent community, or even carving out time for yourself where you can fully unwind without any pressure to perform, these spaces are crucial. They give you the chance to reconnect with who you are, to take off the mask and simply *breathe.* In these spaces, you can be honest about your needs, your quirks, your strengths—without the fear of judgment.

But most importantly, give yourself *permission* to be authentic, even in small doses. If you're used to masking, letting your real self out can feel vulnerable, even risky. Start small. Maybe it's letting a close friend see a little more of your true personality, or being honest about how you're feeling instead of defaulting to the typical "I'm fine" response. Over time, you'll build confidence in being authentic, and you'll start to recognize that your real self is just as valuable—more valuable—than the mask.

The Long-Term Benefits of Authenticity

Here's the truth: living authentically is liberating. It's exhausting trying to be something you're not all the time. The more you allow yourself to be real, the more energy you reclaim. The anxiety, the doubt, the exhaustion—they start to fade when you're not constantly in performance mode. And something amazing happens when you stop masking as much: people start to see *you.* The real you.

When you're authentic, the connections you make with others are deeper. Sure, not everyone will accept your true self—and that's okay. The people who matter will, and those relationships will feel more genuine, more fulfilling. You won't be stuck wondering if they like the "real you" or the version of you that you've been pretending to be. There's power in that, in knowing that you're loved and accepted for who you truly are.

And here's something else: the more you practice authenticity, the more you show the world that it's possible to be different and still belong. By being yourself, you pave the way for others who are struggling with masking, showing them that it's okay to show up as they are. You create ripple effects that go beyond your own experience.

So yes, masking has its place. But authenticity? That's where the real magic happens.

Navigating Relationships with Neurotypical People

Relationships can be tricky terrain for anyone, but when you're neurodivergent, navigating friendships, social invitations, and romantic partnerships with neurotypical people can feel like trying to solve a puzzle where the pieces keep changing shape. Neurotypical expectations often don't align with how we naturally function, leaving us wondering if we're doing something wrong, missing cues, or just not fitting in. The truth is, there's no one "right" way to be in a relationship, but understanding some of the differences in how neurotypicals approach connections can make things smoother.

Understanding Neurotypical Friendships

Here's a reality that might resonate: neurotypical people often equate friendship with regular interaction, especially things like hanging out, small talk, and check-ins. For them, friendship is frequently built on casual social interaction—the kind where you text about random things or meet up just to "catch up." The problem? For many of us neurodivergent folks, these social rituals can feel unnecessary, draining, or even confusing.

If you've ever found yourself thinking, *Why do we need to talk about the weather or what we had for dinner?* you're not alone. Small talk isn't just boring for some neurodivergent individuals—it can feel like a chore, a socially prescribed obligation that takes up precious energy. We'd rather dive deep into meaningful conversations or share space without the pressure to constantly fill it with words. This doesn't mean we don't care about our friends, it just means we value quality over quantity when it comes to interaction.

That said, neurotypical people often view consistent interaction as a sign of connection. If you disappear for too long or don't participate in those check-ins, they might assume something's wrong. It's not unusual for neurotypical friends to interpret silence as distance, when for you, it might just be a way to recharge. This disconnect can cause misunderstandings, but there are ways to manage it.

What can help? Communication. Be upfront about how you function in friendships. Explain that just because you're not constantly texting or chatting doesn't mean you're not invested in the friendship. Let your friends know that you value the relationship but may need different rhythms to keep it healthy. Something as simple as saying, "Hey, I might not reach out often, but I'm still here and I care," can go a long way in maintaining a connection without sacrificing your need for space.

Handling Social Invitations

Now, let's talk about the landmine that is social invitations. If you've been on the receiving end of an invite to a party, event, or even casual hangout, you might know the feeling—part excitement, part dread. For many neurotypical people, extending invitations is a polite gesture, something they do because it's expected in their social circles. But here's the catch: they don't always expect you to say yes.

Neurotypical people often invite others to social gatherings as a formality. Sometimes they genuinely want you to be there, but other times, it's more about maintaining social etiquette. The tricky part for neurodivergent individuals is figuring out when an invitation is sincere and when it's more of a social nicety. Over time, this uncertainty can create anxiety: *Do they really want me to come? Will they be upset if I don't?*

Here's what you need to know: It's okay to say no. Learning when and how to decline social invitations without feeling guilty is key to maintaining your mental health. You don't owe anyone an explanation if you're feeling overwhelmed or simply don't have the energy to engage. Neurotypical people often understand that not every invite will be accepted, and if they don't, that's a reflection of their expectations, not your worth.

That being said, if you're unsure whether an invitation is something you can skip, a good strategy is to ask questions. If you feel comfortable, check in with the person who invited you. Something like, "Is this something you really want me to join, or is it more of a general invite?" can help clarify whether your presence is truly important. You'd be surprised how many times the response will be, "Oh, it's no big deal if you can't make it," relieving some of the pressure.

Neurotypical Expectations in Romantic Relationships

If friendships can be confusing, romantic relationships with neurotypical partners add another layer of complexity. Here's where things get challenging: neurotypical partners often bring with them a set of expectations about how relationships "should" work, especially when it comes to communication, emotional expression, and shared experiences.

One major area of potential misunderstanding comes from how we process and express emotions. Neurotypical partners might expect frequent verbal affirmations or regular expressions of affection to feel connected. For neurodivergent individuals, those same expressions might feel overwhelming or unnecessary. It's not that you don't love or appreciate your partner—it's that you may express it differently. You might show love through actions or quiet presence, rather than words. But neurotypical partners might interpret that silence as distance or indifference.

Another common disconnect is around personal space and alone time. Neurotypical people often expect partners to spend a lot of time together, and they might view needing space or silence as a sign that something's wrong. In reality, for neurodivergent people, needing space isn't about pushing someone away—it's about self-regulation. You might need quiet time to recharge, to process your thoughts, or simply to exist without external stimuli. But without clear communication, your neurotypical partner might not understand this need and could take it personally.

The solution here is *open communication*. Talk about your needs upfront. It's important to frame these conversations in a way that helps your partner understand where you're coming from, without them feeling like they're being shut out. For example, instead of saying, "I just need to be alone," try explaining, "Sometimes I need quiet time to recharge, and it helps me be more present with you when we are together." This way, your partner knows that your need for space isn't about them, but about your self-care.

Another area to explore is sensory sensitivity. For many neurodivergent people, things like physical touch, loud environments, or strong smells can be overwhelming. Your partner might interpret reluctance to engage in certain physical activities—whether it's hugging, holding hands, or even being in loud places—as rejection. It's important to explain that sensory overload doesn't reflect how you feel about them; it's about how your brain processes stimuli. Offering alternatives—like suggesting quieter settings or explaining what kind of physical touch feels comfortable—can help bridge that gap.

Here's something else to keep in mind: many neurotypical partners aren't aware of the concept of *masking*. If you've been masking parts of yourself to fit into the relationship, over time, it can lead to resentment or emotional exhaustion. It's crucial to have honest conversations about masking, letting your partner know that while you've adapted in some ways to meet their expectations, it's draining, and you need space to be authentic. The right partner will not only understand but will support your efforts to be yourself in the relationship.

Building Mutual Understanding

The bottom line with all relationships, whether friendships or romantic ones, is that they require understanding and compromise on both sides. Neurotypical people might come into relationships with a default set of expectations that can feel overwhelming or confusing, but that doesn't mean you have to meet them halfway all the time.

It's about balance. Part of navigating these relationships is teaching neurotypical people how to meet *you* where you are too. This might involve educating them about your needs, your sensitivities, and your boundaries. The more honest and upfront you are, the more likely you'll be able to create relationships that aren't just based on performance or adaptation, but on mutual respect and understanding.

The Lifelong Process of Learning and Adapting

Let's get real: navigating neurotypical spaces is *never* a one-and-done situation. It's not like you read a guide, absorb a few tips, and suddenly you've mastered the whole thing. No—this is a *lifelong* process, full of trial and error, misunderstandings, small wins, and plenty of growth. For some of you, a lot of what we've covered so far might feel basic, like you're thinking, *"Yeah, I've been through this already."* For others, this might be hitting exactly where you are right now, feeling like you're just starting to decode the unspoken rules of neurotypical environments. Either way, the journey doesn't end here—whether you're ready for advanced insights or just beginning to connect the dots.

The truth is, not every neurodivergent person's experience lines up neatly with what I've been talking about, and that's okay. My examples come from what I've lived, but your life might play out differently. What's important is that you keep exploring, not just to figure out how you fit into neurotypical spaces, but to discover what resonates most with *your*experience. If nothing has hit home yet, I guarantee you there's someone out there navigating exactly what you're going through—and by continuing to seek understanding, you'll find them.

Unspoken Rules Everywhere

One of the hardest things about living in a world designed for neurotypicals is that so many of the "rules" are unspoken. Neurotypical people seem to just *know* how to act in certain situations, how to respond in conversations, when to speak and when to stay quiet—and you might find yourself constantly wondering, *"How do they all know this stuff?"*

The reality is, these unspoken social rules are everywhere. From the workplace to casual social settings, there's this invisible guidebook most neurotypicals follow. For example, when someone says, "Let's get together sometime," is that an actual invitation? Or is it just a polite way to say goodbye? The line between real intention and social formality can be so blurry that it leaves you in a fog of confusion, constantly guessing what's expected.

Here's where it gets tricky: not every situation has a clear right answer. Some moments might require you to adapt and mask to get through it, while others might offer you a chance to be more yourself. There are no hard and fast rules for when to do what. And that's frustrating, I know. But part of this lifelong process is learning to read these moments and make decisions on a case-by-case basis. Sometimes, you'll get it right. Other times? Not so much. But the important thing is that you're learning and refining your understanding along the way.

The goal isn't to become a perfect social chameleon. It's about finding what works for *you*, recognizing when it's worth adapting to neurotypical norms and when it's okay to stand firm in your own way of doing things. You're not aiming for perfection, you're aiming for balance.

Building Resilience

Let me be blunt: you're going to make mistakes. We all do. In fact, a lot of us neurodivergent people go through life feeling like we're making more mistakes than everyone else. You might misread a social cue, react too intensely to something, or feel completely overwhelmed by an environment that everyone else seems to handle just fine. It's all part of the process, and the only way through it is to build *resilience*.

Resilience is about bouncing back. It's knowing that just because you stumbled today, that doesn't mean you've failed. Each time you misinterpret a situation or feel like you didn't handle something the "right way," that's an opportunity to learn—not a reason to beat yourself up. But let me be clear: resilience doesn't mean pushing yourself to constantly adapt or conform until you're exhausted. It's about staying open to growth, learning from each experience, and forgiving yourself when things don't go as planned.

There will be moments when you feel completely out of your depth—like everyone else got a handbook for navigating the world and you didn't. But what neurotypicals don't always talk about is that *they* make mistakes too. The difference is that their mistakes might be more easily forgiven or understood within their social framework. Our missteps, on the other hand, can feel amplified because we're already outside the norm. That's why resilience is so important.

Resilience is also about trusting your own process. Some days, you might feel like you're getting nowhere. On other days, you'll feel like you're making massive strides in understanding how to handle different situations. Both are part of the journey, and both are valid. Stay patient with yourself—resilience isn't just about bouncing back; it's about recognizing that *this is a marathon, not a sprint*.

Maintaining Authenticity While Navigating Neurotypical Spaces

Now here's the heart of it: navigating neurotypical spaces without losing yourself. This is the tightrope you'll walk for life, and it's tricky as hell. You're balancing two worlds—the one you live in, and the one where neurotypical expectations dictate how you should behave. The danger is that, in adapting too much, you start losing sight of who you really are. But the other extreme—refusing to adapt at all—can leave you feeling isolated or excluded from the very spaces you want to be a part of.

So, how do you maintain your authenticity while still functioning in a neurotypical world? First, it's crucial to recognize that being *you* is not just acceptable, it's essential. Your neurodivergent mind has strengths that are powerful and unique, and those don't need to be hidden away to make others comfortable. But I also get that this world wasn't built with us in mind, so understanding how to strike that balance—when to adapt and when to stand firm—is the lifelong challenge.

Pick your battles. This phrase has been around forever, and for a good reason. There will be times when masking or adapting to neurotypical norms is necessary. Maybe you're at work, in a meeting, or dealing with a high-stakes situation where the risk of being misunderstood is too great. In those moments, choosing to mask or play by their rules might be the best option, not because you're giving up your authenticity, but because you're strategically navigating a world that doesn't always make space for you.

But—and this is important—*know when to take the mask off.* Know when to give yourself permission to be fully you. Surround yourself with people who get it, who don't need you to hide or adapt. Find communities where your authentic self is celebrated, not tolerated. And within those spaces, be unapologetically you. That might mean creating boundaries, explaining your needs, or simply letting others in on the fact that you experience the world differently. The more you find these moments of authenticity, the more balanced your life will feel.

Give yourself grace. You're not going to get it right every time. Some days, you'll feel like you've compromised too much, and other days, like you've resisted when you should've adapted. But that's okay. This is a lifelong process, and you're learning with every step. Staying true to yourself doesn't mean rejecting every neurotypical expectation—it means knowing which ones serve you and which ones don't.

Moving Forward: Research and Exploration

If you're looking for more advanced strategies, there's plenty out there to explore. What I've shared so far reflects my experiences, but every neurodivergent person has their own path. You might find that some of the most helpful tools come from books, articles, or communities where people are sharing what works for them. Keep digging, keep asking questions, and keep learning. There's no single blueprint for navigating this world as a neurodivergent individual—but there are endless ways to find what works best for you.

Whether you're here for the basics or ready for the next level, remember that this journey is about progress, not perfection. Keep your curiosity alive. Stay open to learning. And most importantly, honor who you are throughout it all. You're not just learning to adapt to a neurotypical world—you're learning to thrive in it, without losing what makes you exceptional.

MENTAL HEALTH; IT MATTERS.
Chapter 5

In late 2019, I stumbled across this thing called "crypto art." Back then, it was still finding its identity, slowly transforming into what people now call NFTs. I've always had a knack for spotting trends before they take off—things that don't quite fit into the mainstream but have a way of sticking with me. So, I dove in. I started making art just for the sake of it, and that was cathartic in a way I hadn't felt in a long time. Art became my release, a way to express all the things that didn't fit into words. But as much as I loved creating, it was lonely work. Most people weren't interested yet, and the few who were tended to keep to themselves.

Then, 2020 hit, and everything changed. I'd gone from startup life, where the pace matched my own rhythm, to a job that required day-to-day office life. It felt like a cage, honestly. I didn't last long there. I'd been open about my autism from the beginning, even tried explaining some of my quirks when I felt it was necessary—like how my brain worked, how I'd pick up on things differently, and how I sometimes needed space to refocus. But it didn't seem to matter. The day they let me go, the owner looked me straight in the eye and said, "You want me to understand how your brain works, but you can't seem to understand how everyone else's works."

I just looked back at him and said, "Yeah, that's called a disability."

All I'd wanted was a little understanding, but his realization had come far too late. I'd spent so much time and energy masking—hiding the very best parts of myself—just to survive in that environment. I'd been pushing down the traits that made me who I am, all for a paycheck. And in hindsight, being let go was such a blessing. It was freeing, but not without its own kind of pain. At that moment, I saw clearly just how much I'd been masking, performing, and adapting myself to fit into places I didn't belong.

It wasn't easy. I'd already been through some rough years—I'd just exited a business acquisition, dealt with illness, and now I was out of a job in the middle of a pandemic. So, I went home that day and made myself a promise. I would focus on building my own business. I'd find ways to work with clients that appreciated what I could bring to the table, and I'd dig into the creative consulting work that actually meant something to me.

As I started to rebuild, I found myself on Clubhouse—a platform where, suddenly, everyone was craving connection. The brightest minds, the most influential voices, they were all there, talking, sharing, building something new. It was weirdly perfect timing. While everyone else was isolated, I was traveling, experiencing this strange, lonely freedom, masking my own feelings and throwing myself into hours upon hours on Clubhouse. I hosted rooms, made connections, helped artists release their NFTs. I've always loved public speaking, so holding these "drop party" rooms for artists felt natural. Sometimes I'd keep a room open for eight hours, just letting people come in, share their stories, talk about their art. It was crazy how speaking into my phone could connect me with people from all over the world.

Eventually, I started thinking about creating my own NFT collection. But I wanted it to have purpose—I wanted it to support autism research. I knew my brain was different, and I knew there were so many of us out there, living lives no one quite understood. Adults with autism have been overlooked for so long, and I wanted to change that. So, I started this project called "Double Pops." It was a simple idea: pixelated popsicles, each one unique. I figured it could be a way to explain autism to kids. Each popsicle looked different, but they were all popsicles at their core. Maybe it was a stretch, but at the time, it felt right. A lot of my artist friends jumped on board, creating their own versions, and we decided a portion of the proceeds would go to charity.

But there was one problem—I had no relationship with any autism organization. I didn't even know how I was going to donate cryptocurrency, but I was determined to make it happen. I reached out to the Southwest Autism Research and Resource Center (SARRC) and told them about the project. I told them I had thousands of dollars waiting to be donated. They were amazed. They took my suggestion to connect with an organization that could help them onboard crypto donations, and that's where it all began. And as the project took off, I did something I'd never done before: I started owning my diagnosis and publicly stated that I was autistic. I put it in my social bios and made it known that anyone who wanted to talk could reach out. I started having incredible conversations, hours-long exchanges with people who just wanted to understand themselves better.

From 2020 to now, I've helped over 1,200 adults either seek their own diagnosis or feel more comfortable self-identifying. As I got deeper into the world of autism and neurodiversity, I realized something else: when you spend enough time learning about the way different minds work, you start to recognize patterns in others. You start to see the signs, and it makes you wonder just how many of us there are out there, hidden in plain sight, masking just to get by.

I'll never forget meeting Daniel Openden, the president of SARRC. We sat down for breakfast in this busy part of Phoenix, where I had to blend in, mask everything, just to make it through. But as we talked, I realized that he'd spent a lot of time around autistic adults. I told him about masking, about how I'd trained myself to look people in the eye for just the right amount of time, glance away, then look back, so I'd seem "normal." I explained how I'd learned to balance sensory input—how I'd focus on looking at the ground so I could actually listen to the conversation, or divert my attention away from expressions and body language because they were often louder to me than the words themselves. He listened, and then he told me I didn't have to mask around him. But what I wanted him to understand was that I *had to*. It wasn't for him; it was for me. It's become my armor, the thing I put on to get through the day, something I can finally take off when I'm home, alone, letting myself stim out all the energy I'd held in.

That conversation led him to invite me to join a new board of self-advocates, a group of autistic adults helping SARRC shape their initiatives. At the first meeting, I walked in, looked around, and saw other people who were more visibly autistic than I was. For a moment, I felt like an outsider, like I didn't belong. But as we started talking, I realized something profound: these people were just like me. I noticed traits in them that I shared, things I did at home, in my own space, when I was free to just *be*. And it hit me—I was home.

In that room, I let go. I looked at the floor, rocked back and forth when I needed to, and spoke up when it felt natural, not worrying if it was "the right time." It was liberating in a way I'd never experienced. I decided that day I would devote myself to helping others who've been hiding, who've been told to silence the parts of themselves that don't fit. Because if I've learned anything, it's that embracing who you are can change your life. It changed mine, and now, every time I see someone find that same freedom, it makes all the struggles, all the masking, worth it.

After that meeting, I felt like I'd unlocked a part of myself that had been buried under years of trying to fit into spaces that weren't made for me. Suddenly, I didn't feel the need to hold back. For the first time, I realized that being true to myself, in all my neurodivergent glory, wasn't just okay—it was necessary. And that revelation brought a clarity I hadn't felt before.

That project with the Double Pops became more than just art. It was a statement. People connected with it, and I stopped questioning my ideas and started believing in them. Before long, I pitched an entirely new project to a celebrity group, and that idea grew into a multimillion-dollar initiative that kept my company busy for two years. And what was even more remarkable was that through that work, I discovered my own art style, generating hundreds of thousands of dollars in sales.

Fast forward to April 2024. I'd partnered with SARRC on something I never would have dreamed of: an autism awareness license plate for the state of Arizona. I was there when the governor signed it into law, standing next to the art I'd created, knowing that $17 from each plate sold would go directly to support autism research. That plate might raise millions for neurodiversity research, all because I'd taken that first step toward embracing who I really was.

Now, don't get me wrong—I still struggle. I go to work each day, knowing I'll need to compose myself, to mask certain behaviors, to be "professional" in a world that doesn't often leave room for the kind of thinking I do. But I'm open about who I am. I talk less about the "disability" and more about the identity. And it's given me a kind of confidence I never had when I was just trying to blend in.

I recognize, too, that I'm in a position many don't have the privilege of being in. There are people out there who don't get the choice to mask or unmask—they just survive however they can. I have so much respect for those individuals because I know what it's like to feel the weight of your own mind every day. And just because I'm able to navigate the neurotypical world doesn't mean I don't need support or community. In fact, the more I've embraced who I am, the more I want to connect with others who feel like they're on the outside looking in.

Neurodiversity isn't a new thing. It's been with us from the beginning. The way I see it, we're just now beginning to recognize it, like buying a new car and suddenly seeing that model everywhere. It's what they call the Baader-Meinhof phenomenon. Once you become aware of something, you start to see it all around you. And that's how I feel about neurodiversity—it's not that there are suddenly more of us, it's that we're finally being seen. We're finally starting to see each other.

And I truly believe neurodivergent minds are exceptional. I look at some of the greatest thinkers, the most influential leaders, and I see the traits I've come to understand as neurodivergent. It's the quirks, the relentless drive, the unconventional thinking—all things that make people say, "Wow, they're a genius," when in reality, they're just wired differently. We're not here to blend in; we're here to make people see the world in a new way. I'm convinced the exceptional have always been neurodivergent.

So, yeah, every day is still a balancing act. I'm aware of the parts of me that need to be contained in certain settings and the parts I let loose when I'm alone. But I've found my voice, and I'm going to use it to help others find theirs. I know what it feels like to be misunderstood, to be told you're "too much" or "not enough." And if I can help even one person step into their identity with confidence, then it's all worth it.

If you're reading this and you're still searching for that acceptance, let me tell you—it's out there. It might not look the way you expect, and it might take longer than you'd like, but you'll find it. There are people who will appreciate you for everything you are, not just the parts you've polished to fit in. It took me years, but I found my people. I found a way to bring my whole self to the table, and now I'm creating spaces where others can do the same.

And if you're in a position to advocate for yourself, do it. But remember, there are those who can't. There are people who need extra support, who need voices like ours to amplify their needs. If we can bridge that gap, if we can connect and support each other, we can build a world where neurodiversity is celebrated, not just tolerated. I believe neurodiversity is the new exceptional—and we're just getting started.

What you think and feel, matters.

The mental health challenges that neurodivergent individuals face aren't just about dealing with anxiety, burnout, or feeling like an outsider—they're deeply connected to the constant act of masking.

Masking is something many of us do so often, so naturally, that we sometimes don't even realize it's happening. It's part of how we navigate a world that doesn't fully understand us, and while it may help us blend in, it comes at a cost. In this section, we'll dig into what masking really is, why it's so exhausting, and how to start recognizing when it's happening. This is the first step toward reclaiming the parts of yourself that have been buried under years of adaptation.

Defining Masking

Let's start with the basics: what is masking, exactly? Masking is the process of adapting behaviors to fit into neurotypical norms, hiding parts of ourselves that we've learned aren't "acceptable" in certain settings. It's suppressing natural expressions, movements, or interests just to avoid standing out or being labeled "different."

For instance, maybe you naturally avoid eye contact because it feels too intense, but in a work setting, you force yourself to look people directly in the eye because you've learned that's what's expected. Or perhaps you've mastered the art of small talk, nodding along, laughing when it feels right, and saying just enough to seem engaged, even though the conversation feels like it's draining your soul. Over time, these little changes build up until they become an invisible mask you wear every day, hiding the real you.

Masking isn't just about acting a certain way in social settings; it can also mean hiding interests or passions that might seem "too much" for others. It's holding back on talking about something you're intensely interested in because you've been told it's "weird" or "obsessive." It's filtering out your natural responses to things because you've learned that what feels right to you doesn't match what's "normal."

In short, masking is a way of adjusting, blending, and, ultimately, hiding parts of yourself to fit into a world that doesn't always make space for you. And while masking can help you get through the day, the cumulative effect of constantly pretending to be something you're not can be devastating.

Masking as Survival

The reason so many neurodivergent individuals mask is simple: survival. From a young age, we start picking up on social cues and learning that certain behaviors make us stand out. We learn that "normal" looks a certain way, and if we want to avoid rejection, judgment, or misunderstanding, we'd better do our best to mimic that.

Think about the times when you've been in a new job, at a party, or just navigating a grocery store and felt that pressure to act a certain way. Masking starts as a defense mechanism. You learn to blend in because standing out comes with risks—risks of being misunderstood, risks of being dismissed, and risks of being labeled as "weird" or "difficult."

The story we explored earlier touched on a moment where I felt that pressure to mask in a work setting. I'd been open about my neurodivergent traits, but when I was let go, it became painfully clear that my efforts to explain myself hadn't bridged the gap. It's moments like that which drive the need to mask, to hide parts of yourself, even when it doesn't feel right. Masking is about trying to fit into a mold that doesn't quite fit, and while it may seem to help in the short term, the long-term impact on mental health is profound.

Masking also shows up in relationships and friendships. We learn to suppress certain traits or behaviors because we're afraid of losing connections. Maybe you've forced yourself to engage in small talk, even though it feels superficial, because you don't want to seem rude. Or perhaps you've toned down your passion for a particular subject because you've been told it's "too much" or "too intense." Each time we mask, we're doing it to survive in a world that's constantly telling us we're not quite right as we are.

Mental Health Implications of Masking

Masking doesn't come without a cost. It takes an enormous toll on mental health, affecting everything from our sense of identity to our energy levels. Living behind a mask means you're always "on," always performing, and that kind of constant vigilance is draining. Here's how it affects our mental health:

- **Burnout**: Masking is mentally, emotionally, and physically exhausting. Imagine going through every interaction, every conversation, monitoring yourself to make sure you're not saying or doing anything that might stand out. It's like running a marathon every day. Burnout isn't just about being tired; it's about being depleted. When you're constantly suppressing who you are, it wears you down over time. The exhaustion from masking can hit so hard that you find yourself unable to engage with anything, even things you love. That's what burnout from masking looks like—a complete and total depletion.

- **Anxiety**: Masking breeds anxiety. You're constantly second-guessing yourself, wondering if you're getting it "right." Am I looking at them enough? Am I talking too much? Should I be laughing here? It's a cycle of self-monitoring that leaves you feeling tense, worried, and hyper-aware of every little thing you say or do. And because anxiety often feeds on uncertainty, masking creates a loop where you're always questioning whether you're fitting in, whether you're being "normal" enough, and whether people are seeing through the mask.

- **Identity Confusion**: One of the most insidious effects of masking is the way it erodes your sense of self. When you spend so much time pretending to be something you're not, you start to lose track of who you really are. You find yourself asking, *Am I doing this because I want to, or because I've learned it's expected?* Masking can lead to a profound sense of identity confusion. You spend so much time wearing the mask that eventually, you start to forget what it's like to live without it.

- **Isolation**: Masking often creates a deep sense of isolation. You may be surrounded by people, but if they only ever interact with your masked self, it's hard to feel truly connected. The relationships you build while masking can feel shallow because they're not with the real you—they're with the version of you that's trying to fit in. This can lead to feelings of loneliness and disconnection, even when you're not technically alone.

The longer you mask, the heavier these effects become. You might even start to believe that the masked version of you is all there is. It's why so many neurodivergent individuals struggle with self-esteem and self-worth, questioning whether they're "enough" just as they are. The mental health toll of masking isn't just about feeling exhausted—it's about losing touch with yourself and wondering if you'll ever find your way back.

Realizations about Masking

One of the most important steps toward reclaiming your authentic self is to start recognizing the moments when you find yourself masking. It can be difficult at first—masking is often something we do automatically, without even thinking about it. But becoming aware of those moments is the first step to understanding how masking impacts your mental health and how you can begin to reclaim the parts of yourself you've hidden away.

Here are a few questions to ask yourself when you're reflecting on a day or an interaction:

- *When did I feel the need to adjust my behavior?* Start noticing the situations that bring out the mask. Is it at work? With certain people? In certain social settings?

- *What specific behaviors am I changing?* Maybe it's suppressing stimming, holding back on talking about your interests, or forcing yourself to engage in small talk. Recognize the patterns.

- *How did it feel afterward?* Notice the mental and emotional impact of masking. Did you feel drained, disconnected, or anxious? Did you feel like you were holding back pieces of yourself?

Once you start recognizing these moments, you can begin to make conscious choices about when and where you want to mask. Masking may be necessary in certain settings, but it doesn't have to be an all-or-nothing deal. You can find safe spaces where you don't have to hide, places where you can start to unmask and feel the relief of being your true self.

Masking doesn't have to define you. It may be a tool you use, a strategy for navigating a world that wasn't built for you, but it doesn't have to consume you. By becoming aware of when and why you mask, you take the first step toward reclaiming the parts of yourself that you've tucked away. The more you can do that, the more you'll discover that your true self is worth bringing to the surface, no matter what the world might say.

The Weight of Neurotypical Expectations on Mental Health

One of the biggest challenges for neurodivergent individuals in a neurotypical world is the constant pressure to adapt to expectations that aren't designed for us. It's a silent, often invisible strain, one that can lead to deep-seated anxiety, lingering feelings of isolation, and ultimately, burnout. Nowhere is this pressure felt more intensely than in the workplace.

In a work environment, the stakes feel especially high. You're there to get things done, to prove yourself, to fit into a culture that you don't get to shape—at least, not right away. Employers want to see results; they want to support productive employees, but they're less inclined to invest in supporting someone who hasn't yet "proven" themselves. So, you end up in this strange position of needing to mask, to blend in just enough to be accepted, until you've established yourself enough to feel secure in your role. Only then, if you're lucky, do you get to show a little bit more of who you really are.

The mental health impact of this constant adaptation can be profound. Neurotypical expectations are woven into every aspect of work culture, from the small talk at the start of the day to the "right" way to conduct a meeting. Let's explore some of the specific ways that meeting these expectations impacts mental health and talk about strategies for managing those effects.

Anxiety from Social Expectations

Anxiety is often the first thing that bubbles up when you're trying to conform to a world that operates on neurotypical social norms. From the moment you walk into a workplace, there are unspoken rules and hidden cues that everyone else seems to just *get*. But for us, it's like trying to navigate a labyrinth with no map. The smallest interactions become big mental hurdles: *Did I make eye contact for too long? Am I talking too much? Should I even be talking at all?*

Workplaces can be particularly intense because, often, you're expected to participate in behaviors that don't come naturally. Whether it's forced small talk before a meeting, navigating office politics, or trying to "sound confident" when speaking up in a meeting, each one of these demands takes energy—energy spent second-guessing every little thing. And when you try to be open about your neurodivergent needs, sometimes it feels like that honesty is met with a blank stare or, worse, an outright dismissal. You might be told that "it's just the way things are here," and suddenly, your needs feel like burdens.

But in those early days, masking often feels essential. You need to demonstrate that you're capable, that you can fit in and deliver what's expected of you. Employers, at this stage, are still assessing you, and in many cases, they aren't ready to accommodate until they "know" you. It's a vicious cycle: you have to mask to fit in, and the more you mask, the more anxiety builds. You're always in a state of hyper-awareness, constantly scanning for signals, constantly adapting, and constantly wondering if it's enough.

Depression from Loneliness and Isolation

The longer you're in environments where masking is necessary, the easier it is to start feeling isolated. Even if you're surrounded by people, that sense of loneliness can creep in when you realize you're not truly seen. In the workplace, this isolation is often amplified. You may be able to connect with colleagues on a surface level, but when masking is your default mode, the relationships you build don't feel as real. It's like you're on one side of a glass wall, watching everyone else engage with each other in a way that feels natural to them but just beyond your reach.

Despite the connections you might form online or in neurodivergent-friendly communities, there's often an underlying sense of disconnection that lingers. At work, everyone's bonding over shared experiences that don't quite resonate with you. They talk about social events you have no interest in, make casual jokes that fly over your head, and build rapport in ways that feel foreign. Even if you're included, there's a feeling that you're only partway there, always a little bit removed, a little bit on the outside.

This can lead to a form of depression that's less about sadness and more about a numbness, a sense of being disconnected from the world around you. You're showing up, doing what's expected, but it doesn't feel fulfilling or meaningful. You start questioning whether there's a place for you at all, whether you'll ever find a way to feel connected in a world that seems to operate on a different frequency.

Burnout as a Result of Over-Accommodation

When you're constantly adapting to neurotypical norms, especially in a work setting, burnout becomes almost inevitable. It's not just about working long hours or tackling challenging tasks—it's about the *extra* energy spent trying to fit in. You're not just showing up to do your job; you're showing up to manage other people's perceptions of you, to meet unspoken expectations, and to maintain a performance that doesn't come naturally. All of this adds up, leaving you mentally and physically drained.

In the story, there was a moment of profound relief when I finally found myself in a room of other autistic adults, where I didn't have to mask. I could stim, look away, and be present without worrying about whether I was conforming to someone else's standards. That moment was liberating, but it also highlighted just how exhausting it had been to hold it all in, day after day, in environments where masking felt like the only option.

Burnout from over-accommodation isn't something that a good night's sleep can fix. It's a depletion that goes beyond physical fatigue, touching every part of your being. It's when you've spent so much time trying to be someone else that you've run out of energy for even the smallest tasks. The cumulative effect of always being "on" is unsustainable, and burnout is the body's way of signaling that something needs to change.

Strategies for Coping

While the weight of neurotypical expectations is heavy, there are ways to manage the mental health impact. Here are some strategies for navigating environments that demand constant adaptation:

- **Set Clear Boundaries**: In the workplace, setting boundaries can be tricky, especially when you're new and trying to fit in. But even small boundaries can help protect your mental health. If you need quiet time, try scheduling your breaks in a way that lets you recharge away from others. If small talk feels overwhelming, look for ways to gracefully disengage when possible.

- **Practice Selective Masking**: Masking is often necessary to some degree, but it doesn't have to be an all-or-nothing approach. Identify situations where you can afford to let the mask slip a bit, like during breaks or in more casual interactions. Save your energy for the times when masking is absolutely essential, and let yourself relax a little in moments where the stakes aren't as high.

- **Recognize Early Signs of Burnout**: Pay attention to your body and mind. If you start noticing that you're feeling more fatigued, irritable, or disengaged, take it as a sign that you might be heading toward burnout. Take these signs seriously, and don't ignore them in the hope that they'll go away. Adjust your workload, reduce non-essential tasks, or take breaks where you can.

- **Seek Support When Possible**: If you've been at your job for a while and feel secure enough, consider having an honest conversation with a trusted colleague or supervisor about your needs. You may be surprised at how supportive people can be once they understand what you're dealing with. In some cases, advocating for yourself can lead to accommodations that make a real difference in your daily experience.

- **Create Personal Rituals to Decompress**: After a long day of masking, take time for activities that help you shed the accumulated stress. This could be stimming, diving into a favorite hobby, going for a quiet walk, or anything that helps you reconnect with yourself. Think of it as a way to re-center, to reconnect with the parts of you that have been hidden throughout the day.

- **Connect with Others in Similar Situations**: When possible, build a support network of other neurodivergent individuals who understand what you're going through. Whether it's an online community or a local advocacy group, having people who "get it" can be incredibly validating. They can offer advice, share coping strategies, and remind you that you're not alone in your experiences.

Constantly navigating neurotypical expectations, especially in environments like the workplace where you have little control, can be overwhelming. But by setting boundaries, practicing selective masking, and prioritizing your mental health, you can find a balance that allows you to meet your needs and fulfill your role. The more you understand your own limits, the better equipped you'll be to manage these expectations without losing yourself in the process.

Next, we'll explore how reclaiming authenticity can transform not just how you feel, but how you relate to the world around you. As we dive into the concept of unmasking and building connections with others, you'll find ways to reconnect with your identity and begin creating spaces where you're free to be fully yourself.

Reclaiming Your Authentic Self

Masking is survival. For neurodivergent people, it's what we do to get through situations where standing out isn't an option. But here's the problem: hiding your true self chips away at your identity. And after a while, you don't just forget who you are—you get used to pretending that you're someone else. It's time to change that. Reclaiming your authentic self is a process of unlearning, reconnecting, and letting go of the need to meet neurotypical expectations. It's not about indulging in "self-care" or easing into a new mindset; it's about taking intentional, strategic steps to show up as *you*—unfiltered and unapologetic.

Recognizing When You're Masking

The first step in reclaiming your authentic self is knowing when you're hiding it. If you're not sure when you're masking, here's the truth: you're probably masking more often than you realize. Start paying attention to situations where you feel like you have to put on an act. Are you changing your tone? Holding back? Forcing yourself to engage in pointless small talk? Each of these signals that you're hiding pieces of yourself to fit in.

Here's the deal: if you don't start identifying those moments, you'll never break the habit. Next time you feel yourself "switching on" in public, ask yourself:

- *What am I censoring right now?* Whether it's stimming, avoiding eye contact, or forcing a laugh, know what behaviors you're changing.

- *Who or what is triggering this?* Is it a specific person, a place, or a type of interaction?

- *Why am I masking?* Are you doing it out of fear, habit, or because you've been told it's necessary? Challenge that reason.

Once you know where your masking habits show up, you can begin to dismantle them. You have to see the mask to take it off.

Steps to Unmasking

Don't make the mistake of thinking unmasking means dropping every social filter you've built up over the years. This is about *controlled* unmasking—finding places and people where you can start showing your true self in small but powerful ways. It's about learning to let the guard down, not for everyone else's comfort, but for your own sanity.

Here are a few ways to get started:

1. **Identify Your Safe Spaces**: Pick environments where the stakes are low. Maybe it's with a friend who "gets" you, or an online group where neurodivergent people can be themselves. These are the places to start experimenting with unmasking because they offer room to breathe.

2. **Choose One Behavior to Unmask**: Don't overwhelm yourself by trying to drop every mask at once. Pick one behavior to stop suppressing. If it's stimming, let yourself stim when you need to in these low-stakes settings. If it's avoiding eye contact, give yourself permission to look away and focus on the conversation instead. Unmasking in layers will allow you to build confidence without feeling exposed.

3. **Practice Selective Authenticity in New Situations**: This isn't about flipping a switch. Start testing small bits of authenticity in unfamiliar spaces, like speaking up a little more directly at work or sharing a genuine opinion without filtering it. You don't need to unleash your entire personality in one go. Make unmasking a strategy, not a performance.

4. **Expand Gradually**: The more you unmask in comfortable settings, the easier it becomes to unmask elsewhere. You don't have to stay in "safe spaces" forever. Take your authenticity out into the world, little by little. The more you let yourself show up as you are, the less you'll care about how it's received.

Building Self-Compassion

The reality is that unmasking is risky. You'll face judgment, and you'll get pushback—sometimes from people you care about. But here's where you need to understand: building self-compassion isn't about babying yourself. It's about having your own back, about knowing that the opinions of others don't change your value.

Self-compassion is critical. If you mess up or find yourself slipping back into masking, don't waste time beating yourself up. Accept it, adapt, and move forward. Unmasking is a process. It doesn't mean you have to like every step of it, but you do have to respect yourself enough to keep going.

- **Celebrate Progress, Not Perfection**: Progress means you're on the right track. Maybe you unmask around a new group and get a few weird looks. Good. That's a sign you're pushing past comfort zones. If you let yourself take pride in these moments, you're building resilience, not just confidence.

- **Cut Off Negative Self-Talk**: If you find yourself doubting whether unmasking is "worth it," ask yourself what the alternative is. Do you want to go back to hiding? Let yourself feel the discomfort of being real. It's better than the slow suffocation of living a lie.

Embracing Sensory Needs and Stimming

Part of reclaiming your authenticity means acknowledging your sensory needs. If stimming helps you stay grounded, it's time to stop seeing it as something to hide. Neurotypical people fidget, pace, or shake their legs all the time, and no one bats an eye. Stimming is just your version of that.

Reintegrate stimming and other sensory needs into your life as a practice. Don't hold back just because you're in public. Start letting yourself stim in ways that work for you, and push back on the idea that it's something you need to hide. Here are some ways to incorporate your sensory needs into daily life without apology:

- **Create Your Own Sensory Space**: Designate a spot where you can engage in sensory activities. Whether it's using fidget tools, a weighted blanket, or something tactile, make that space yours and use it unapologetically. This is where you can decompress and reconnect with yourself.

- **Bring Sensory Comforts with You**: When you're in a setting where you can't fully stim, bring small items that let you engage subtly. Carry a fidget toy, chewable jewelry, or a textured fabric that you can discreetly use to ground yourself.

- **Stim Freely in Trusted Environments**: When you're with people who accept you, let yourself stim without holding back. It's a way of saying, *This is who I am.* Don't apologize for it. If others feel uncomfortable, that's their reaction to manage—not yours.

- **Communicate Your Sensory Needs When Necessary**: You don't owe anyone an explanation, but if you feel like sharing, let others know how sensory experiences impact you. Tell them that stimming isn't optional for you—it's essential. The more you communicate this, the more you'll find people willing to understand and respect it.

The reality is that reclaiming your authentic self requires action, not just intention. It means you'll have to get used to some discomfort, and you'll likely have to face parts of yourself you've hidden for too long. But the reward? A life that feels like it belongs to you. You'll know that each time you unmask, you're not just existing—you're living in a way that's real, a way that doesn't ask you to cut away pieces of yourself to fit in.

The world won't always accommodate you, but that's not your problem to fix. The only thing you need to focus on is creating a life where *you* don't have to mask. Embrace who you are, live unapologetically, and let others deal with the discomfort of seeing a version of you that doesn't conform. Because this is your life, and every time you choose authenticity over hiding, you're choosing a life that's yours in a way masking never could be.

The Power of Finding Your Community

Isolation can be brutal. Living in a world where neurotypical norms dominate can make you feel like you're always on the outside looking in. But finding your community? That's game-changing. When you connect with people who *get* you—people who've experienced the same struggles, faced the same misunderstandings, and learned to thrive anyway—you're not just finding friends; you're reclaiming a sense of belonging. This section will explore the impact of finding your community and how it can transform everything from your mental health to your self-acceptance.

Why Community Matters

The truth is, neurodivergent people are often forced to exist in a world that doesn't meet them halfway. You spend years learning to mask, to downplay your natural traits, and to mold yourself into something that fits into neurotypical spaces. But when you finally find a group of people who reflect the same qualities you've kept hidden, something powerful happens.

In that moment, you realize that you're not alone. You start to see that the behaviors you've been suppressing aren't "weird" or "wrong"—they're completely natural. You're not the only one who feels overwhelmed by sensory input or prefers direct conversation over small talk. When you see others unapologetically stimming, being blunt, or taking sensory breaks, it gives you permission to do the same. You start to see that the parts of yourself you've hidden aren't flaws; they're simply expressions of who you are.

Community matters because it takes away the pressure to conform. When you're with people who understand your experience, you don't have to justify your actions or explain your behavior. There's an unspoken understanding, a shared language. You're no longer constantly on edge, worried about judgment or misunderstanding. Instead, you can just *be*, and that's something we're rarely given the freedom to experience.

Online and In-Person Communities

Finding the right community doesn't have to mean upending your entire life. The beauty of the internet is that there are now countless spaces where neurodivergent individuals can connect and support one another. Here are some starting points for finding your own community:

- **Online Platforms**: Places like X (twitter), Clubhouse, Discord, and Reddit are full of groups focused on neurodivergent experiences. Search for channels and rooms dedicated to autism, ADHD, dyslexia, and other forms of neurodiversity. These spaces are often open 24/7, allowing you to connect with people across time zones, share your thoughts, and learn from others who've been where you are.

- **Specialized Social Media Groups**: Facebook groups, Instagram communities, and even LinkedIn have spaces where neurodivergent individuals share stories, resources, and support. Look for groups focused on neurodiversity advocacy, adult autism, or whatever area resonates with you. These spaces can be a great way to get support in real-time.

- **Local Advocacy Groups**: Check your area for neurodiversity-focused meetups or advocacy groups. Organizations like the Autism Society and other local advocacy groups often host in-person meetings, events, or workshops. Being able to connect face-to-face can take your sense of community to a whole new level. If you're not sure where to start, try Meetup.com or search for neurodiversity organizations in your area.

- **Virtual Conferences and Webinars**: With more events moving online, you can attend conferences, workshops, and webinars focused on neurodiversity. These events aren't just about learning—they're opportunities to connect with others who share your experiences. Many of these events offer networking sessions, breakout rooms, or Q&A segments where you can meet others on the same journey.

The key is to find spaces that resonate with you, spaces where you feel welcomed and understood. You don't have to join every community you come across; find one or two that feel genuine and invest your energy there. It's about quality over quantity.

One strong connection with someone who *gets it* can be worth more than a hundred surface-level interactions.

Balancing Support with Boundaries

Community is essential, but it doesn't come without its challenges. Just because someone shares neurodivergent traits doesn't mean they're automatically a perfect fit for you. It's okay to be selective about the people you allow into your life. Prioritize connections that are supportive, respectful, and uplifting.

Here's the reality: boundaries are necessary, even within your community. Not every neurodivergent person will mesh well with you, and that's okay. You're allowed to protect your energy. If you find that certain interactions leave you feeling drained or if someone's approach clashes with your values, it's perfectly acceptable to step back. You don't owe anyone unlimited access to your time or emotional energy.

A few key things to remember as you navigate boundaries in your community:

- **Check In with Yourself Regularly**: After spending time in a community space or interacting with someone, take a moment to assess how you feel. Are you energized? Drained? Feeling empowered? If certain spaces or people consistently leave you feeling off, that's a sign to reevaluate those connections.

- **Prioritize Positivity and Respect**: Connect with people who support you and encourage you to embrace your authentic self. It's not about surrounding yourself with yes-men; it's about finding people who challenge you constructively and respect your boundaries.

- **Don't Feel Obligated to Share Everything**: Just because you're part of a community doesn't mean you have to lay out every detail of your life. Share what feels comfortable, and hold back on things that feel too personal or vulnerable. It's okay to take your time and build trust slowly.

Finding a community is about building a support system, not creating new obligations. The right people will understand and respect that. Healthy boundaries ensure that your connections remain sources of strength, not stress.

Giving Back and Advocating for Others

Once you find your community, there's another layer of connection that can bring an even greater sense of purpose: advocacy. Giving back to your community doesn't have to mean grand gestures or major projects. It can be as simple as sharing your story, offering advice, or supporting someone who's just beginning their journey.

Advocacy is about making sure other neurodivergent people feel seen, heard, and valued. It's about creating spaces where everyone can experience the same freedom you've found. When you share your story, when you step up and say, "This is who I am, and I'm not changing that for anyone," you're doing more than helping yourself—you're paving the way for others.

Your journey might inspire someone who's struggling to find their footing, someone who's just beginning to unmask, or someone who's feeling lost in a world that doesn't understand them. Use your experience to give back, whether it's through direct advocacy, community projects, or even small acts of support.

Here are some practical ways to start advocating for others:

- **Mentor Someone New**: If someone in your community reaches out for guidance, consider offering your insight. Share the lessons you've learned, the tools that have helped you, and the mistakes you've made along the way. Sometimes, having a single person to turn to can change someone's entire outlook.

- **Organize Meetups or Discussion Groups**: If you're comfortable, consider creating spaces where others can connect. This could mean hosting virtual meetups, organizing online discussion groups, or planning a local gathering. These spaces don't have to be elaborate; just a place where people can share experiences and feel understood.

- **Support Advocacy Projects**: If you're in a position to start a project that benefits the neurodivergent community, go for it. Whether it's a fundraiser, an awareness campaign, or a creative initiative like the autism awareness license plate project, there are countless ways to give back. Use your strengths, your voice, and your resources to make a tangible impact.

- **Be Visible and Vocal**: Sometimes the simplest way to advocate is by living openly and unapologetically. Add neurodivergent identifiers to your profiles, speak out on social media, and make it known that you're someone others can connect with. Visibility matters—it lets others know they're not alone.

Finding community isn't just about finding people who accept you; it's about joining forces with people who have walked a similar path, people who can help you move forward. And once you're part of that community, there's an opportunity to help others find their way too. Advocate, give back, and lift others up. This is the power of community—it's not just about connection, but about creating a network of support and strength that amplifies all of our voices.

Because when we stand together, unashamed and unfiltered, we're no longer isolated. We're no longer just surviving in a world that wasn't built for us. We're thriving, unapologetically, on our own terms.

Discovering Your Unique Strengths and Purpose

Here's the reality: discovering your unique strengths and purpose is not a passive process. It's not about waiting for a spark of inspiration or hoping the world will reveal your path. It's about relentless pursuit, constant effort, and getting to know yourself in a way that most people never bother to. You have to dig deep, figure out what drives you, and then put in the work to make that passion meaningful—not just for you, but for the world around you.

If you think you can simply "believe" your way into a life of purpose, you're kidding yourself. Purpose doesn't just happen because you want it to; it's something you have to make happen. It requires you to take ownership of your strengths, no matter how unconventional, and use them in ways that make an impact. Every successful project, every meaningful moment, is the result of a thousand small actions, a hundred decisions to show up, and a commitment to keep pushing forward, even when it's uncomfortable.

Let's break down how you can take that drive, that fire, and turn it into something real.

Embracing Special Interests

The first step is understanding that your passions—your deep, sometimes obsessive interests—are worth pursuing. These interests aren't just hobbies or distractions; they're clues to what makes you unique. For me, it was crypto art and NFTs. I had a natural instinct for spotting trends, and I threw myself into a space that felt fresh, creative, and filled with potential. That passion became a bridge to something bigger. It was more than just art—it became a way to connect with people and to start conversations that mattered.

So ask yourself: *What do I care about? What makes me feel alive?* If you're not sure, that's fine. Start paying attention to what draws you in, to the things you think about when you're supposed to be doing something else. Don't apologize for these interests, and don't hold back. The world will try to tell you to pick a safer path, to go for something more conventional. Ignore that. You have one life, and no one else gets to decide what you should be passionate about.

Exploring and Honing Skills

Once you've identified what interests you, it's time to get to work. Passion without skill is a dead end, so you need to invest in honing those interests into abilities that make a difference. Just liking something isn't enough—you have to become good at it. You have to put in the hours, the effort, the trial and error, to turn your interest into expertise.

When I started the Double Pops project, it was just a simple idea: pixel art that could explain autism to kids in a way that made sense. But it wasn't just about drawing or selling art. I researched, networked, and figured out how to turn that project into something meaningful. I took my interest and made it practical. I found ways to connect it with a cause I cared about, to transform it from a project into a purpose.

Whatever it is that excites you, take it and make it yours. Build skills around it. Learn everything you can, experiment, and take risks. Push yourself to create something you can be proud of, and don't wait for permission. Permission is a waste of time. Just start.

Turning Your Interests into Advocacy

Here's where things get powerful. Once you've found a passion and you're good at it, start thinking about how you can use it to make a difference. You have a unique perspective, and the world needs that perspective. There are countless ways to take what you love and turn it into advocacy, into something that serves a cause bigger than you.

The autism awareness license plate project? That wasn't about me making art. It was about using my skills to create something that raised awareness and generated funding for autism research. It was about taking something I loved and making it matter. Look at your own passions and think about how they intersect with issues you care about. Whether it's art, writing, technology, or something else, there are ways to make it serve a bigger purpose.

This doesn't have to be some grand, multi-year project. Advocacy can start small. Maybe it's using your voice to educate people, creating content that raises awareness, or volunteering your skills to an organization that needs them. The important thing is that you don't let your interests stop at self-satisfaction. Take that passion and channel it into something that impacts the world around you. That's where purpose really starts to take shape.

Finding Self-Worth Through Purpose

Aligning your strengths and passions with a purpose isn't just about achieving external goals—it's about building a sense of self-worth that can't be easily shaken. When you know what you stand for and you're actively pursuing it, you're not just living; you're thriving. You have a direction, a sense of why you're here, and that clarity is priceless.

Your purpose becomes a foundation. It's something you can rely on when everything else feels uncertain. When you're rooted in purpose, the opinions of others lose their power over you. You're no longer living for anyone else's approval because you're doing something that matters to you. You're choosing your own path, on your own terms, and that is where true self-worth is built.

But understand this: purpose isn't a one-time decision. It's not a set-and-forget kind of deal.

Purpose is something you have to commit to, day after day. It's a series of actions, choices, and habits that keep you aligned with what matters. There will be days when you question if it's worth it, when you wonder if you're making a difference at all. That's normal. The key is to keep moving forward, to keep showing up, and to remind yourself that every step counts, even when progress feels slow.

Action Steps: Defining Your Strengths, Passions, and Purpose

This process is about taking ownership of your strengths and finding ways to make them count. It's not about finding a quick fix or expecting instant clarity. It's about doing the work, diving deep, and allowing yourself to connect with the parts of you that matter most. The following steps will help you get clear on what drives you, what you're good at, and how to put those pieces together into something meaningful.

Step 1: Identify Your Core Interests and Passions

Start by getting clear on the things that *truly* interest you. This isn't about what you think you *should* care about or what others have told you is "worthwhile." It's about finding the things that resonate with you on a deep level.

Make a Passion Inventory: Set aside some uninterrupted time and make a list of the activities, topics, or areas you're drawn to. Write down anything that comes to mind, without judgment. Don't filter yourself; let it flow.

Ask Yourself Why: For each item on your list, dig deeper. Why does it matter to you? What draws you to it? The more you understand the *why* behind your interests, the more you'll be able to connect them to a greater purpose. For example, if you're fascinated by art, think about what it is about art that speaks to you—maybe it's the creative expression, the connection with others, or the way it makes you feel free.

Rank Your Interests: Go through your list and rank each item in order of importance. Think about what makes you excited to learn more, what you lose track of time doing, and what you'd still be interested in even if no one else ever knew about it. Pick the top three items from your list—these are likely your core passions.

Step 2: Define Your Strengths and Skills

Next, identify the strengths you already have and the ones you're willing to develop. This step is about acknowledging what you're good at *now*, as well as recognizing areas where you can grow.

Write Down Your Current Skills: Start by listing the skills you have right now. Include both "hard" skills (like writing, coding, or public speaking) and "soft" skills (like listening, problem-solving, or empathy). Don't be modest here; list everything that comes to mind, no matter how minor it might seem.

Look for Patterns: Once you have your list, look for themes. Are there skills that align with the passions you identified in Step 1? For example, if you're passionate about art and also skilled at digital design, you're already seeing a natural fit. Circle or highlight any skills that directly connect with your top three interests.

Identify Areas for Growth: For each passion you identified, think about the skills you'll need to make an impact in that area. If you want to make a difference in environmental conservation, maybe you need to learn more about communication to effectively spread awareness. Write down the skills you're willing to commit to developing and start making a plan to build them up.

Step 3: Connect Your Passions and Strengths to a Purpose

Now that you've identified your interests and strengths, it's time to start connecting them to a purpose. This isn't about picking a random cause and diving in; it's about aligning your passions with something meaningful.

Explore Potential Causes and Issues: Take your top interests and think about areas where they can make a difference. If you're into technology, maybe it's creating accessible tools for neurodivergent individuals. If you're passionate about music, consider teaching music to underserved communities. List a few possible causes or issues that resonate with you.

Choose One Area to Focus On: You don't need to save the world overnight. Pick *one* cause that aligns with both your passions and strengths. It should be something that gets you excited, something that you can start contributing to right away. Remember, this is just a starting point; you can expand from here as you gain experience.

Define Your Contribution: Get specific about how you'll make an impact. What role do you want to play? Are you interested in advocating, creating, organizing, or teaching? Outline one or two tangible ways you can start contributing. If your passion is art, maybe your contribution is creating a series of pieces that highlight a cause you care about. If it's advocacy, maybe you begin by raising awareness through social media or volunteering with a relevant organization.

Step 4: Set Realistic Goals and Take Immediate Action

It's not enough to have a plan—you have to *act*. This step is about breaking down your goals and taking concrete steps forward.

Set Three Actionable Goals: Based on your purpose, set three short-term goals that you can realistically accomplish within the next month. For example, if your focus is on advocacy, your goals might be to (1) research organizations that align with your purpose, (2) attend a local meeting or webinar on the topic, and (3) create a small project (like a blog post, piece of art, or video) that raises awareness about your cause.

Establish a Routine: Make your purpose a part of your daily life. Set aside time every day, even if it's just 15 minutes, to work on one of your goals. Consistency is what will keep you moving forward, even when progress feels slow. It's the repeated actions, day in and day out, that build momentum.

Hold Yourself Accountable: Tell someone you trust about your goals and ask them to check in with you. You don't need a cheerleader; you need accountability. Share your progress regularly, and if you start slipping, remind yourself why you're doing this. Purpose requires discipline, and accountability will help you stay on track.

Step 5: Reflect and Refine Your Path

As you make progress, take time to reflect on what you're learning and adjust your course as needed. Purpose is not static. It evolves as you evolve, and it's essential to stay flexible while staying committed.

Evaluate Your Progress Weekly: At the end of each week, reflect on what you've accomplished, what challenges you faced, and how you can improve. Ask yourself if your actions are moving you closer to your goals. If they're not, figure out what needs to change.

Stay Open to New Opportunities: The more you commit to your purpose, the more opportunities will begin to show up. Keep an open mind and be willing to pivot if something aligns with your goals and passions in an even bigger way. Just make sure any changes keep you aligned with what you care about.

Adjust Your Goals and Keep Moving: As you achieve your initial goals, set new ones. Purpose isn't a one-and-done deal; it's a constant evolution. Revisit these action steps regularly, and continue to challenge yourself. Purpose will continue to unfold as you deepen your commitment to the things that matter most.

Purpose is something you create through sustained effort, dedication, and the willingness to push past comfort zones. It's not something you stumble upon; it's something you *make* happen. By defining your interests, honing your skills, aligning with a cause, and taking consistent action, you're not just discovering purpose—you're building it from the ground up.

The work won't always be easy, and there will be times when you question whether it's worth it. But remember: purpose is the thing that makes every struggle meaningful. Keep pushing forward, and you'll find that each step brings you closer to a life that feels undeniably yours.

Wake-Up Call: Are You Really Going to Take Action?

Here's the hard truth: reading this won't change anything. You can absorb every word, nod along, feel motivated, and still walk away without making a single change in your life. So ask yourself: *Are you going to take action, or are you just going to read this, feel inspired for a moment, and then move on like you always have?*

Are you going to *do* the work, or are you just hoping that one day, somehow, things will fall into place? It's time to face a tough question: *Are you ready to be honest about the patterns that hold you back?*

For many of us, executive dysfunction is the enemy. It's the thing that keeps you stuck, watching opportunities pass you by while you sit there wishing things would change. It's the voice that says, "I'll get to it tomorrow," or, "Maybe later, when I feel more ready." But here's the thing: *tomorrow never comes if you're always waiting to feel ready.*

The only way out of this cycle is to take action *now*. And it doesn't have to be huge—it just has to be real. You have to wake up, face your habits, and commit to doing things differently. This isn't about waiting for motivation. It's about building habits that make action automatic, even when you don't feel like it. If you're serious about living a life of purpose, it's time to RISE.

RISE: Recognize, Inspire, Support, Empower

This isn't just a feel-good acronym. It's a daily checklist for building a life that you're in control of. If you're tired of drifting, if you're done waiting, then it's time to start showing up for yourself in a way that matters. Here's how you can RISE every day:

Recognize Your Issues: Start by calling out the habits and patterns that are keeping you stuck. Be brutally honest with yourself. Are you procrastinating? Are you making excuses? Are you telling yourself that you're too tired, too busy, or just not ready? Recognize these thoughts for what they are: obstacles. Identify your biggest roadblocks and name them.

Inspire Yourself: Motivation doesn't just show up; you have to find ways to trigger it. Remind yourself daily *why* you're doing this. What are you fighting for? Who do you want to become? Surround yourself with reminders of your goals. Write them down, put them where you'll see them, and use them to fuel your actions. Inspire yourself by staying focused on the *vision* of where you're going, and don't let yourself lose sight of it.

Seek Support (or Support Yourself): You don't have to go at this alone. Look for people, groups, or resources that can offer guidance, accountability, and encouragement. Find someone you can share your goals with, someone who will push you to keep going when you're ready to quit. And if support isn't available, then be your own backup. Create structures that hold you accountable. Set alarms, track your progress, write in a journal—do whatever it takes to keep yourself on track.

Empower Yourself Every Day to Get Shit Done: Empowerment isn't about *feeling* powerful; it's about *acting* powerfully. Take action every single day, no matter how small. Build momentum by making it impossible to go a day without moving forward. Whether it's sending an email, making a list, reaching out to someone, or researching your next step, do something every day that brings you closer to your goals. Empowerment comes from repeated action, not from waiting to feel inspired.

So here's the question again: *Are you really going to take action?* You have everything you need right here to start making things happen. It's time to stop dreaming and start building. RISE up, get out of your own way, and take control. Because without action, nothing changes. And the only person who can take that action is you.

Moving Forward with Confidence and Compassion

You've come a long way in this chapter. You've explored the cost of masking, the weight of neurotypical expectations, and the importance of building a life that's rooted in your unique strengths. But here's the bottom line: you can't afford to stop here. Moving forward with confidence and compassion isn't just about living authentically—it's about taking ownership of who you are, using your voice to create a world where you, and others like you, can thrive unapologetically.

This isn't a quick fix. It's a journey that will require resilience, patience, and a willingness to learn and adapt. But if you commit to it, you'll discover a version of yourself that isn't just surviving but thriving. The process may be ongoing, but with each step, you're building a life that's truly yours.

Normalizing Self-Advocacy

If there's one takeaway here, let it be this: advocating for yourself is not an option; it's a necessity. You have a right to define the conditions you need to succeed. You're not asking for special treatment; you're claiming the space that allows you to show up as your best self. Whether it's in the workplace, in your relationships, or even within your own mind, you have to start setting clear, unapologetic boundaries.

Self-advocacy might feel uncomfortable at first, especially if you're used to masking or downplaying your needs. But every time you advocate for yourself, you're building the foundation for others to do the same. You're sending a message that neurodivergent traits aren't weaknesses—they're strengths that deserve respect. So speak up, ask for accommodations, and let people know what you need. And remember: it's not just for you. Each time you advocate, you're paving the way for others, too.

Embracing Lifelong Growth

The journey to self-discovery doesn't have an endpoint. You're going to evolve, and as you do, your understanding of yourself will deepen. This isn't about reaching a state of perfect self-acceptance and staying there. It's about constantly learning, adapting, and growing into the person you're meant to be.

Embrace the fact that you're always going to be a work in progress. There will be setbacks, days when you doubt everything, and times when you feel like you're starting from scratch. That's all part of the process. Take it one step at a time, and don't rush yourself. Growth isn't linear, and it doesn't need to be. What matters is that you keep showing up, keep learning, and keep pushing forward, even when it's uncomfortable.

Supporting Those Who Cannot Advocate for Themselves

Not everyone has the privilege or the ability to advocate for themselves. Some neurodivergent individuals can't speak up about their needs, and others may be in environments where their voices aren't heard. If you're in a position where you can advocate, consider it a responsibility, not just a choice. Use your voice to create spaces where neurodiversity is respected, not hidden.

You have the unique opportunity to drive change, to amplify the voices of those who aren't able to advocate for themselves. This might mean supporting policies that promote inclusivity, volunteering with organizations that serve neurodivergent communities, or simply being a source of encouragement for others. By using your own journey to raise awareness, you're not only helping yourself but also creating a world that is better for everyone.

Owning Your Identity

At the end of the day, embracing neurodiversity isn't just about you. It's about building a world that values diverse ways of thinking, feeling, and interacting. Owning your identity as a neurodivergent person means refusing to let society's narrow definitions of "normal" define you. It's about standing tall in your uniqueness and letting the world know that neurodivergent minds are exceptional.

You have qualities that others can't even begin to understand. You see things differently, approach problems in ways that break the mold, and possess strengths that most people will never have. That's not something to hide—that's something to celebrate. By embracing your neurodivergent traits, you're not just living authentically; you're helping to build a world that sees and values the exceptional qualities of diverse minds.

So take ownership of who you are. Show up in the world with the confidence that your differences are what make you powerful. And remember, this isn't just about acceptance—it's about pride. When you own your identity, you're not just carving out space for yourself; you're setting a new standard for what it means to be exceptional.

Moving forward, keep this in mind: this journey is about creating a life where you don't have to hide, where you don't have to mask, and where you don't have to apologize for who you are. This journey is about walking into each day with the confidence to show up fully as yourself and the compassion to lift others up as you go.

You're building something powerful here—a life that's yours, shaped by your own terms. Don't settle for anything less.

EXPLORING THE SPECTRUM OF NEURODIVERSITY

Chapter 6

In this chapter, we're going to take a deep dive into the many types of neurodiversity that exist. I've done my best to include every type of neurodivergent condition I could find, from the ones you've probably heard of to those that might be completely unfamiliar. There are conditions here that are widely recognized, as well as others that aren't officially acknowledged by the medical community but are experienced by countless individuals around the world.

Here's the thing: I'm not a doctor, and this chapter isn't meant to diagnose or define anyone's experience. Neurodiversity is an emerging and ever-evolving field, and what I'm presenting here is based on my personal research, anecdotal evidence, and accounts from neurodivergent individuals.

Some of these descriptions may reflect mainstream views, while others represent newer or more niche perspectives. This isn't about creating a definitive guide—it's about opening the door to understanding and exploring the diversity of human minds.

And here's an important point before we dive in: *don't* turn this chapter into a checklist for diagnosing yourself with every neurodivergent trait under the sun. It's easy to read about symptoms and start seeing them in yourself, a phenomenon called hypochondria. Neurodiversity is broad, and while some of these traits may resonate with you, it's essential to take a step back and really evaluate your experiences. Reflect, research, and, if necessary, consult a medical professional.

The goal of this chapter is to help you gain awareness of the many ways neurodivergence can manifest, and to show that each type of neurodiversity has its own unique potential. As you read through, focus on building understanding, not jumping to conclusions. This chapter is about curiosity, respect, and the remarkable diversity of the human mind.

With that said, let's begin our exploration of neurodiversity. I'm going to only list 45 but there are hundreds to be listed. This is just the start to help you understand how vast the diversity spectrum really is. I will also represent potential opportunities these diversities could bring and their potential disabilities.

1. Autism Spectrum Disorder (ASD)

- **Awareness**: Autism Spectrum Disorder (ASD) is a developmental condition that affects communication, social interactions, and behavior. It includes a wide range of manifestations, from mild to more significant challenges, and is unique to each individual.

- **Manifestation**: May present as difficulty with eye contact, repetitive behaviors, intense focus on specific interests, and sensitivity to sensory input. Autistic individuals may struggle with social nuances and communication, though this varies greatly.

- **Disability Potential**: Communication difficulties, sensory overload, and challenges with social interaction can impact daily functioning in neurotypical environments.

- **Opportunity Potential**: Individuals with autism often have strong attention to detail, pattern recognition, and deep focus, making them skilled in fields like technology, research, and the arts.

- **Examples**: An individual who meticulously organizes collections or becomes an expert on a niche topic; someone who finds comfort in routine and may become overwhelmed in unpredictable settings.

2. Attention Deficit Hyperactivity Disorder (ADHD)

- **Awareness**: ADHD is characterized by symptoms of inattention, hyperactivity, and impulsivity. It impacts executive functioning, which includes skills like time management, planning, and impulse control.

- **Manifestation**: May look like daydreaming, restlessness, fidgeting, difficulty focusing on one task, and being easily distracted. ADHD can also involve hyperfocus, where a person becomes intensely engrossed in an activity they enjoy.

- **Disability Potential**: Challenges with organization, maintaining attention on tasks, and meeting deadlines can interfere with academic or work performance.

- **Opportunity Potential**: Individuals with ADHD often excel in dynamic, fast-paced environments. Creativity, quick thinking, and problem-solving skills make them well-suited to careers in entrepreneurship, the arts, and other innovative fields.

- **Examples**: A person who can jump between tasks quickly, thriving in environments that require adaptability; or someone who struggles with sitting still in a traditional classroom setting but lights up in creative or hands-on situations.

3. Dyslexia

- **Awareness**: Dyslexia is a language-based learning disability that affects reading, spelling, and writing. It is unrelated to intelligence and instead reflects differences in how the brain processes language.

- **Manifestation**: Often appears as difficulty decoding words, poor spelling, slow reading speed, and challenges in remembering written information. Dyslexic individuals might find reading exhausting or frustrating but often excel in verbal communication and creative thinking.

- **Disability Potential**: Reading difficulties can impact academic performance, especially in language-heavy subjects. Spelling and writing challenges may lead to difficulties in professional or academic environments.

- **Opportunity Potential**: Dyslexic individuals frequently have strengths in visual-spatial reasoning, problem-solving, and big-picture thinking. They may excel in fields like design, engineering, and entrepreneurship.

- **Examples**: Someone who struggles with reading aloud but has a knack for storytelling, or a person who finds conventional study methods challenging yet shines in hands-on learning environments.

4. Dyscalculia

- **Awareness**: Dyscalculia is a learning disability that affects a person's ability to understand and perform mathematical calculations. It can impact basic arithmetic, number sense, and the ability to learn math-related concepts.

- **Manifestation**: May include difficulty with basic math tasks, understanding numbers, and recognizing numerical patterns. A person with dyscalculia might struggle with telling time, managing finances, or performing simple calculations.

- **Disability Potential**: Math-related tasks can be a barrier in both academic and everyday settings. Challenges with numeracy can make budgeting, measuring, and time management difficult.

- **Opportunity Potential**: People with dyscalculia often have strong verbal skills, creativity, and problem-solving abilities. They may excel in areas like literature, art, and other fields where math isn't the central focus.

- **Examples**: Someone who avoids math-intensive tasks but has a talent for storytelling or visual arts, or an individual who struggles with equations but can articulate complex ideas clearly in other areas.

5. Dysgraphia

- **Awareness**: Dysgraphia is a learning disability that affects writing abilities, including handwriting, spelling, and organizing thoughts on paper. It can impact fine motor skills and written expression.

- **Manifestation**: May look like messy handwriting, poor spelling, and difficulty organizing ideas into coherent written sentences. Writing tasks can feel laborious, and individuals might avoid them as a result.

- **Disability Potential**: Written communication can be a challenge, impacting academic performance and workplace tasks that require extensive writing.

- **Opportunity Potential**: Individuals with dysgraphia may excel in verbal communication, storytelling, or fields that don't rely heavily on writing. They often have strong creative thinking and oral expression skills.

- **Examples**: A person who struggles with taking notes but is an engaging speaker, or someone who prefers visual arts or oral presentations over writing assignments.

6. Dyspraxia (Developmental Coordination Disorder)

- **Awareness**: Dyspraxia, also known as Developmental Coordination Disorder, affects motor coordination and planning, making it difficult for individuals to perform movements smoothly. It can impact both fine and gross motor skills.

- **Manifestation**: Often appears as clumsiness, difficulty with tasks like tying shoelaces or using utensils, and challenges with activities that require precise motor coordination (e.g., writing, sports).

- **Disability Potential**: Physical tasks can be more challenging, impacting daily activities, self-care, and tasks that require fine motor skills. Social interactions may also be affected due to difficulties with activities like sports.

- **Opportunity Potential**: Dyspraxic individuals often excel in creative thinking, empathy, and problem-solving. They may also be particularly strong in areas like verbal communication, art, and innovation.

- **Examples**: Someone who struggles with handwriting but has excellent verbal skills, or an individual who avoids sports but enjoys creative arts or brainstorming sessions.

7. Tourette Syndrome

- **Awareness**: Tourette Syndrome is a neurological disorder characterized by repetitive, involuntary movements and vocalizations called tics. Tics can range from simple movements (like eye blinking) to complex vocal outbursts.

- **Manifestation**: Tics may include facial grimacing, shoulder shrugging, or verbal outbursts. They can be mild or severe and may become more noticeable under stress. While the nature of tics varies, they are generally involuntary and can be difficult to control.

- **Disability Potential**: Tics can impact social interactions and lead to misunderstandings or stigmatization. In some cases, they may interfere with tasks requiring steady, controlled movements.

- **Opportunity Potential**: People with Tourette's often develop resilience, quick thinking, and adaptability. Many have strong verbal and auditory processing skills, which can be advantageous in dynamic fields.

- **Examples**: Someone who uses humor or creativity to manage social situations involving tics, or an individual who channels their energy into public speaking, music, or other expressive outlets.

8. Sensory Processing Disorder (SPD)

- **Awareness**: Sensory Processing Disorder

affects how the brain processes sensory information, leading to hypersensitivity or hyposensitivity to stimuli like sounds, lights, touch, or smells. It's common in autism but can occur independently.

- **Manifestation**: May look like aversion to certain textures, sounds, or bright lights, or alternatively, seeking out sensory input (e.g., craving deep pressure or certain textures). Hypersensitivity might lead to avoidance of crowded places, while hyposensitivity may lead to seeking intense sensory experiences.

- **Disability Potential**: Sensory issues can interfere with daily activities and social interactions, as certain environments may feel overwhelming or uncomfortable. This can make participating in regular activities more challenging.

- **Opportunity Potential**: Individuals with SPD may develop strong sensory awareness and can excel in roles that benefit from attention to sensory detail, such as art, design, or culinary work. They also tend to be empathetic and highly perceptive.

- **Examples**: A person who avoids loud, crowded spaces but creates art with intricate visual details, or someone who finds certain textures soothing and might excel in tactile or hands-on work.

9. Auditory Processing Disorder (APD)

- **Awareness**: Auditory Processing Disorder impacts the brain's ability to interpret sounds, particularly speech. Individuals may hear sounds clearly but struggle to process or understand them, especially in noisy environments.

- **Manifestation**: May look like difficulty following spoken instructions, confusion when distinguishing similar sounds, or needing extra time to respond to verbal cues. This can be mistaken for inattentiveness or hearing loss, though hearing itself is usually normal.

- **Disability Potential**: Challenges with verbal communication and sound interpretation can make classroom learning, workplace meetings, and social interactions more difficult.

- **Opportunity Potential**: People with APD often develop strong visual and spatial skills to compensate. They may excel in fields like art, visual design, or computer programming, where verbal processing isn't the primary focus.

- **Examples**: Someone who relies on written instructions and visual cues, or a person who excels in areas that involve visual problem-solving or hands-on tasks over verbal tasks.

10. Visual Processing Disorder

- **Awareness**: Visual Processing Disorder

affects the brain's ability to interpret visual information, which can impact reading, understanding spatial relationships, and interpreting visual cues. This is distinct from issues with eyesight itself.

- **Manifestation**: May look like difficulty with reading comprehension, navigating spaces, or interpreting maps. A person with this disorder may struggle with visual tasks like puzzles or coordinating visual information with physical actions.

- **Disability Potential**: Reading, driving, and navigating physical spaces can be challenging, especially when detailed visual information is required. It can impact academic performance in subjects that require heavy reading or precise visual processing.

- **Opportunity Potential**: Individuals with visual processing challenges often develop strong auditory and kinesthetic abilities. They may excel in fields like music, storytelling, or sports where vision is less central.

- **Examples**: Someone who prefers listening to audiobooks over reading, or an individual who enjoys hands-on activities like crafting or musical performance, which rely more on auditory and tactile processing than visual processing.

11. Obsessive-Compulsive Disorder (OCD)

- **Awareness**: OCD is a mental health condition involving repetitive, intrusive thoughts (obsessions) and behaviors or rituals (compulsions) meant to reduce the anxiety these thoughts cause. Although OCD is sometimes classified as an anxiety disorder, it involves specific neurobiological differences.

- **Manifestation**: May include repetitive behaviors like handwashing, checking, counting, or ordering objects. Intrusive thoughts might lead to compulsive actions intended to alleviate anxiety. These rituals can take up a significant amount of time and impact daily functioning.

- **Disability Potential**: OCD can interfere with work, relationships, and daily life due to time-consuming rituals and the distress caused by obsessions. Individuals may feel compelled to perform certain actions even when they recognize them as irrational.

- **Opportunity Potential**: People with OCD often have an eye for detail, high levels of focus, and strong organizational skills. Many excel in fields requiring precision, structure, or thoroughness, such as research, data analysis, or quality control.

- **Examples**: Someone who takes extra time to organize items or checks work repeatedly for errors, which can be advantageous in roles where attention to detail is crucial.

12. Bipolar Disorder

- **Awareness**: Bipolar Disorder is

characterized by shifts in mood, energy, and activity levels. These shifts can range from manic episodes (elevated mood, energy, or irritability) to depressive episodes (feelings of sadness, low energy, and hopelessness). It's a mood disorder with clear neurobiological underpinnings.

- **Manifestation**: May include periods of high energy, reduced need for sleep, impulsive decision-making during mania, and extreme fatigue, lack of motivation, or sadness during depression. These cycles can last for days, weeks, or even longer.

- **Disability Potential**: Mood swings can impact relationships, job stability, and personal well-being. The extremes of mood can make it difficult to maintain consistent daily routines or commitments.

- **Opportunity Potential**: Individuals with bipolar disorder may experience periods of intense creativity, productivity, and insight. Many excel in fields that benefit from creative thinking, such as art, writing, or entrepreneurship.

- **Examples**: A person who experiences bursts of creative inspiration during manic phases, leading to unique artistic or professional contributions, followed by periods of rest or low energy.

13. Intellectual Disabilities (ID)

- **Awareness**: Intellectual Disabilities involve limitations in intellectual functioning (reasoning, learning, problem-solving) and adaptive behaviors, impacting daily life, social skills, and practical skills. Intellectual disabilities can range from mild to profound.

- **Manifestation**: Individuals may have challenges with tasks that require complex thinking or adaptive skills, such as managing finances, social communication, or navigating new environments. Support needs can vary widely depending on the severity.

- **Disability Potential**: Daily tasks, academic pursuits, and independent living skills may be more challenging, particularly in areas requiring abstract thinking or complex problem-solving.

- **Opportunity Potential**: Individuals with intellectual disabilities often excel in tasks with clear, structured steps and predictable patterns. Many are capable of developing deep, meaningful relationships and can thrive in roles that emphasize routine and reliability.

- **Examples**: A person who enjoys tasks that involve repetition or hands-on activities, excelling in roles where these traits are valued, such as hospitality, assembly work, or caring for animals.

14. Learning Disabilities (General)

- **Awareness**: Learning Disabilities are a category of neurodiversity that includes challenges in specific academic areas, such as reading, writing, or math. They are processing disorders that impact how individuals understand or use information.

- **Manifestation**: May present as difficulty with reading comprehension, organizing written work, remembering math facts, or following multi-step instructions. Each individual with a learning disability may experience unique challenges based on the specific areas affected.

- **Disability Potential**: Learning disabilities can impact academic achievement, particularly in subjects that require strong reading, writing, or mathematical skills. This can lead to frustration and difficulties in traditional educational settings.

- **Opportunity Potential**: Individuals with learning disabilities often excel in creative and visual-spatial skills. Many are innovative thinkers who thrive in hands-on environments, making them well-suited to roles in the arts, trades, and other practical fields.

- **Examples**: Someone who might struggle with standardized testing but excels in creative projects, or a person who has difficulty with traditional note-taking but is an exceptional problem-solver.

15. Schizophrenia Spectrum and Other Psychotic Disorders

- **Awareness**: This category includes conditions like schizophrenia and schizoaffective disorder, which are characterized by disruptions in perception, thought processes, and emotional regulation. Symptoms may include hallucinations, delusions, disorganized thinking, and impaired social functioning.

- **Manifestation**: Individuals may experience auditory or visual hallucinations, believe things that are not based in reality, or have difficulty organizing their thoughts. Episodes can range in severity and may come and go over time.

- **Disability Potential**: Symptoms can significantly impact daily functioning, relationships, and the ability to work or engage socially. Medication and therapy are often necessary to help manage symptoms and improve quality of life.

- **Opportunity Potential**: Some individuals with schizophrenia spectrum disorders experience heightened creativity and unique perspectives, which can translate into strengths in creative fields such as art, music, and writing.

- **Examples**: An individual who channels their experiences into creative expression, producing artwork or writing that reflects their inner world, or someone who brings a unique, intuitive perspective to problem-solving tasks.

16. Oppositional Defiant Disorder (ODD)

- **Awareness**: ODD is a behavioral disorder often diagnosed in childhood. It's characterized by persistent patterns of angry, irritable moods, argumentative or defiant behaviors, and vindictiveness towards authority figures.

- **Manifestation**: May appear as frequent temper tantrums, refusal to comply with rules, deliberate attempts to annoy or upset others, and frequent anger or resentment. These behaviors can lead to challenges in school and family dynamics.

- **Disability Potential**: ODD can impact academic performance, relationships with peers, and interactions with authority figures. The behavior patterns associated with ODD may lead to conflicts in structured environments like school or work.

- **Opportunity Potential**: Individuals with ODD may develop strong critical thinking and leadership skills when channeled positively.

Many excel in roles that value independent thought, resilience, and determination.

- **Examples**: A child who frequently questions or challenges classroom rules but shows natural leadership in group projects, or an adult who channels defiance into advocacy or activism.

17. Nonverbal Learning Disability (NVLD)

- **Awareness**: NVLD is characterized by strong verbal skills but significant challenges with nonverbal skills, such as understanding social cues, spatial awareness, and visual-spatial tasks. People with NVLD may struggle with coordination and interpreting body language.

- **Manifestation**: May include difficulty with spatial tasks (like navigating or assembling items), struggles with understanding nonverbal social cues, and a tendency to interpret language very literally. Individuals with NVLD may excel in verbal tasks but face challenges with tasks that require visual-spatial reasoning.

- **Disability Potential**: NVLD can impact social interactions, coordination, and tasks that require visual processing, making it difficult to navigate environments that rely on nonverbal cues.

- **Opportunity Potential**: Individuals with NVLD often excel in verbal reasoning, memorization, and academic subjects that rely on written or spoken language. They may thrive in fields that prioritize verbal communication, such as writing, teaching, or public speaking.

- **Examples**: A person who is highly articulate and excels in verbal tests but struggles with tasks like reading body language or spatial reasoning puzzles.

18. Language Processing Disorder (LPD)

- **Awareness**: LPD is a condition that affects how language is processed in the brain. Individuals with LPD may have trouble understanding spoken language, following conversations, or organizing their thoughts into coherent speech.

- **Manifestation**: May look like difficulty following spoken directions, slow processing of verbal information, and trouble finding the right words. LPD can impact both expressive and receptive language abilities, leading to misunderstandings in communication.

- **Disability Potential**: LPD can impact academic and social interactions, particularly in settings that rely heavily on spoken instructions. Difficulty in processing language can lead to frustration and misunderstandings.

- **Opportunity Potential**: People with LPD often develop strengths in other areas, such as visual or kinesthetic processing. They may excel in fields where written or hands-on skills are prioritized over verbal communication.

- **Examples**: An individual who prefers to communicate through writing rather than speaking, or someone who excels in visual arts and hands-on tasks rather than verbal activities.

19. Executive Functioning Disorder (EFD)

- **Awareness**: EFD affects the brain's ability to manage time, plan, organize, and execute tasks. It's often associated with conditions like ADHD and autism but can also appear independently. EFD impacts day-to-day tasks and long-term planning.

- **Manifestation**: May include difficulty with starting tasks, following multi-step directions, staying organized, managing time, and regulating emotions. Individuals with EFD may struggle with procrastination, impulse control, and task completion.

- **Disability Potential**: EFD can interfere with school, work, and daily life due to challenges in organizing, prioritizing, and following through on tasks. This can impact productivity and lead to issues with meeting deadlines.

- **Opportunity Potential**: Individuals with EFD often develop strong adaptability and creativity. They may excel in dynamic environments where flexibility is valued and can bring unique problem-solving skills to unstructured projects.

- **Examples**: A person who struggles with rigid routines but thrives in flexible work environments, or someone who has difficulty with sequential tasks but excels in creative brainstorming sessions.

20. Traumatic Brain Injury (TBI)

- **Awareness**: TBI is a condition caused by an external force, such as a fall or accident, that impacts the brain's function. TBI can lead to various cognitive, emotional, and physical challenges, depending on the area and extent of the injury.

- **Manifestation**: May result in memory issues, concentration difficulties, changes in mood or behavior, and motor skill impairments. TBI symptoms can be mild (like a brief loss of consciousness) or severe (resulting in significant changes in cognition and behavior).

- **Disability Potential**: TBI can impact mobility, cognition, emotional regulation, and other functions. It may lead to challenges in academic or professional settings, as well as affect personal relationships due to changes in personality or behavior.

- **Opportunity Potential**: Some individuals with TBI develop heightened empathy and resilience, and may excel in roles that involve helping others, advocacy, or creative expression. TBI can sometimes lead to increased creativity as the brain rewires.

- **Examples**: An individual who uses their TBI experience to advocate for brain injury awareness, or someone who finds a new creative outlet as a means of expression following changes in cognitive function.

21. Central Auditory Processing Disorder (CAPD)

- **Awareness**: CAPD is a condition where the brain has difficulty processing sounds, particularly speech, even though hearing is normal. Individuals with CAPD may struggle to understand verbal information, especially in noisy environments.

- **Manifestation**: May include difficulty following spoken directions, distinguishing between similar sounds, or understanding speech in crowded or noisy places. People with CAPD may ask others to repeat themselves frequently and may appear to be inattentive.

- **Disability Potential**: Challenges with verbal communication can impact learning and social interactions, making it difficult to keep up with conversations, lectures, or meetings where information is presented verbally.

- **Opportunity Potential**: Individuals with CAPD often develop strong visual processing skills and may excel in roles that require attention to detail and visual-spatial reasoning.

- **Examples**: A person who relies on visual aids to follow directions or someone who is excellent at visual-based tasks but struggles with verbal communication.

22. Visual Snow Syndrome

- **Awareness**: Visual Snow Syndrome is a neurological condition where individuals constantly see static or "snow" in their vision. This condition can also include other visual disturbances like afterimages or light sensitivity.

- **Manifestation**: Individuals may experience visual disturbances such as seeing grainy or "snowy" patterns, trailing afterimages, and increased sensitivity to light. These symptoms are constant and can affect reading, driving, and other daily activities.

- **Disability Potential**: Visual snow can impact concentration, comfort in various lighting conditions, and visual tasks. It may interfere with activities that require clear, uninterrupted vision.

- **Opportunity Potential**: People with Visual Snow Syndrome often develop strong awareness of visual details and adaptability in managing sensory challenges. Many find creative ways to manage symptoms and excel in environments with controlled lighting.

- **Examples**: An individual who becomes adept at creating low-sensory environments for work or someone who channels their experiences with visual snow into creative or digital art.

23. Hyperlexia

- **Awareness**: Hyperlexia is characterized by an advanced reading ability at an early age, often accompanied by difficulties in understanding spoken language and social cues. It is frequently seen in individuals on the autism spectrum.

- **Manifestation**: May include precocious reading skills, such as reading at a very young age, but with challenges in comprehension and understanding complex language or social nuances. Individuals may have strong memorization abilities but struggle with social communication.

- **Disability Potential**: Comprehension challenges can impact academic and social situations, as understanding figurative language or implied meanings can be difficult. This can create barriers in both educational and interpersonal settings.

- **Opportunity Potential**: Individuals with hyperlexia often have strong pattern recognition, memory, and analytical skills. Many excel in academic areas that rely on memorization and written language.

- **Examples**: A child who reads at a young age but struggles to understand abstract concepts or someone who has a talent for memorizing facts but finds social interactions challenging.

24. Synesthesia

- **Awareness**: Synesthesia is a neurological condition where stimulation of one sensory pathway automatically triggers another. For example, individuals may see colors when they hear music or associate certain tastes with specific words.

- **Manifestation**: Can include experiences such as seeing colors when hearing sounds, feeling textures when reading numbers, or tasting flavors when reading words. This experience is involuntary and consistent for each individual.

- **Disability Potential**: While not usually disabling, synesthesia can sometimes make it challenging for individuals to differentiate between sensory inputs. It can be overwhelming in environments with strong sensory stimuli.

- **Opportunity Potential**: Synesthetes often have strong creative abilities and may excel in fields like music, art, and design, where their unique sensory experiences provide inspiration and enhance their work.

- **Examples**: A musician who creates compositions based on colors they see when hearing notes or an artist who paints using colors they associate with specific sounds or emotions.

25. Aphantasia

- **Awareness**: Aphantasia is a condition where individuals are unable to visualize images in their mind's eye. People with aphantasia may be unable to conjure mental images of people, places, or objects, even if they can describe them in detail.

- **Manifestation**: May look like an inability to picture scenes, faces, or objects in one's mind, even though individuals can describe them conceptually. People with aphantasia often use different strategies for recalling memories or thinking about concepts.

- **Disability Potential**: Aphantasia can impact tasks that rely heavily on mental imagery, such as visualization-based learning, creative writing, or design. However, this can vary greatly depending on the individual.

- **Opportunity Potential**: People with aphantasia often excel in analytical and factual processing and may develop strong verbal and conceptual reasoning skills. Many are excellent problem-solvers and strategic thinkers.

- **Examples**: A person who describes things in logical or factual terms rather than visual detail, or someone who excels in areas where abstract or conceptual thinking is valued over visualization.

26. Hyperphantasia

- **Awareness**: Hyperphantasia is the opposite of aphantasia; it involves exceptionally vivid and detailed mental imagery. Individuals with hyperphantasia can visualize scenes, people, and objects in their mind with extraordinary clarity.

- **Manifestation**: May include a rich, detailed imagination, where mental images are so vivid they're nearly lifelike. People with hyperphantasia can often recall memories in great detail or picture new ideas with ease.

- **Disability Potential**: Although not typically disabling, vivid mental imagery can sometimes lead to sensory overload or make it difficult to distinguish memories from current experiences. In some cases, it may contribute to intrusive thoughts or vivid nightmares.

- **Opportunity Potential**: Individuals with hyperphantasia often excel in creative fields that benefit from strong visualization, such as writing, art, design, or architecture. They may also have strong memory recall due to detailed mental imagery.

- **Examples**: An artist who creates detailed visual artwork from mental images, or a writer who vividly describes scenes and characters with rich sensory details.

27. Highly Sensitive Person (HSP)

- **Awareness**: The term Highly Sensitive Person describes individuals who experience heightened sensitivity to sensory stimuli, emotional cues, and environmental changes. HSPs process sensory information more deeply than average.

- **Manifestation**: May include sensitivity to bright lights, loud sounds, or strong smells. HSPs may also have intense emotional responses and are often very attuned to the moods and emotions of others, making them highly empathetic.

- **Disability Potential**: Sensory and emotional sensitivity can make it difficult to function in crowded or high-stimulation environments. HSPs may become easily overwhelmed in noisy or chaotic settings, impacting social and work-related interactions.

- **Opportunity Potential**: HSPs often excel in fields that require empathy, attention to detail, and sensitivity to subtleties, such as counseling, teaching, or the arts.

Their heightened awareness can make them perceptive and compassionate listeners.

- **Examples**: A person who thrives in one-on-one interactions but avoids crowded events, or someone who notices and responds to subtle changes in people's emotions, making them effective in supportive roles.

28. Misophonia

- **Awareness**: Misophonia is a condition where certain sounds trigger intense emotional reactions, often anger, irritation, or anxiety. Common triggers include sounds like chewing, tapping, or breathing.

- **Manifestation**: May appear as strong, negative reactions to specific sounds that others may not notice. Misophonic individuals may avoid certain environments or need to wear earplugs or headphones to block out triggering sounds.

- **Disability Potential**: Misophonia can interfere with daily life, as individuals may avoid social situations or public spaces where triggering sounds are likely. This can impact relationships, work environments, and overall quality of life.

- **Opportunity Potential**: Individuals with misophonia often develop strong self-awareness and coping strategies. Many are attuned to subtle sound details, which can be beneficial in fields like music, audio engineering, or environmental science.

- **Examples**: A person who works in a quiet environment to avoid triggers, or someone who develops sound sensitivity into a talent for audio-related tasks, such as music production or sound design.

29. Dysphasia (Aphasia)

- **Awareness**: Dysphasia, or aphasia, is a language impairment affecting the ability to produce or comprehend language. It is often a result of brain injury or neurological events like a stroke and can affect spoken and written communication.

- **Manifestation**: May include difficulty finding words, constructing sentences, or understanding language. Dysphasia can range from mild to severe, with some individuals able to communicate effectively in certain contexts but struggling in others.

- **Disability Potential**: Language impairments can significantly impact communication, making it difficult to participate in conversations, express thoughts, or understand others. This can affect social interactions, academic performance, and employment.

- **Opportunity Potential**: Some individuals with dysphasia develop creative ways to communicate, such as through visual arts or music. They may also find meaning and fulfillment in advocacy roles or through storytelling in nonverbal forms.

- **Examples**: An individual who paints or draws to express themselves when language is challenging, or someone who advocates for communication accessibility after experiencing dysphasia themselves.

30. Dysmusia (Amusia)

- **Awareness**: Dysmusia, also known as amusia, is a condition that affects musical processing, making it difficult to recognize tunes, tones, or rhythms. People with amusia may have trouble singing, remembering melodies, or distinguishing between different musical notes.

- **Manifestation**: May include difficulty recognizing familiar songs, inability to carry a tune, or challenges with rhythm. People with dysmusia may avoid music or musical settings due to frustration or lack of enjoyment.

- **Disability Potential**: While not typically disabling in daily life, dysmusia can limit participation in musical activities or impact enjoyment of music. This condition may affect tasks requiring musical skills, such as learning an instrument or engaging in group singing.

- **Opportunity Potential**: Many individuals with dysmusia develop strong skills in non-musical areas, such as visual arts, literature, or science. They may have heightened abilities in areas unrelated to music, allowing them to excel in fields that don't rely on musical perception.

- **Examples**: Someone who finds enjoyment in art, literature, or science instead of music, or a person who appreciates other forms of expression, such as dance or painting, as alternatives to musical participation.

31. Highly Superior Autobiographical Memory (HSAM)

- **Awareness**: HSAM, or Highly Superior Autobiographical Memory, is a condition where individuals can recall nearly every detail of their lives with incredible accuracy. This goes beyond typical memory, allowing them to remember specific dates, events, and personal experiences in vivid detail.

- **Manifestation**: People with HSAM can recall past events, dates, and experiences as if they happened yesterday. This includes minute details of daily life, sometimes going back decades. They can often tell you what they wore, ate, or experienced on any given date.

- **Disability Potential**: While HSAM might sound advantageous, it can be overwhelming. Reliving painful or stressful memories in high detail can lead to emotional strain, anxiety, or difficulty moving on from past events.

- **Opportunity Potential**: Individuals with HSAM often excel in fields that value historical accuracy, personal storytelling, or detailed record-keeping. They may also find unique opportunities in research, psychology, and autobiographical writing.

- **Examples**: A person who can accurately describe events from decades ago, down to specific details, or someone who uses their memory skills to work in historical documentation, research, or biographical writing.

32. Alexithymia

- **Awareness**: Alexithymia is a condition where individuals have difficulty identifying and describing their emotions. People with alexithymia may struggle to put feelings into words or understand the emotions of others.

- **Manifestation**: May include challenges with expressing emotions, understanding why they feel a certain way, or recognizing emotional cues in others. This can sometimes be mistaken for lack of empathy, but it is actually a difficulty with emotional processing.

- **Disability Potential**: Alexithymia can impact social relationships and personal well-being. Difficulty recognizing and processing emotions may lead to misunderstandings in relationships or challenges with emotional regulation.

- **Opportunity Potential**: Individuals with alexithymia often develop strong logical reasoning and may excel in fields that prioritize objective analysis, such as engineering, research, or technical fields.

- **Examples**: A person who is highly analytical but has trouble discussing feelings, or someone who focuses on practical solutions rather than emotional responses.

33. Prosopagnosia (Face Blindness)

- **Awareness**: Prosopagnosia, also known as face blindness, is a condition that affects the ability to recognize faces. People with prosopagnosia may have difficulty identifying even familiar faces, relying on other cues to recognize people.

- **Manifestation**: Individuals may not recognize friends, family, or colleagues by their faces alone and instead use features like voice, clothing, or context to identify others. This can make social interactions challenging and may lead to misunderstandings.

- **Disability Potential**: Prosopagnosia can lead to social anxiety, misunderstandings, and embarrassment, as individuals may fail to recognize people they know well. It can impact personal and professional relationships.

- **Opportunity Potential**: People with prosopagnosia often develop strong skills in recognizing voices, mannerisms, or contextual clues. Many excel in auditory processing, pattern recognition, or verbal skills, compensating for their challenges with face recognition.

- **Examples**: An individual who remembers others by their unique voice or movement patterns, or someone who is adept at picking up other non-visual cues in social settings.

34. Savant Syndrome

- **Awareness**: Savant Syndrome is a rare condition where individuals have extraordinary abilities in specific areas, such as memory, music, math, or art, often alongside developmental or neurological differences.

- **Manifestation**: People with Savant Syndrome may have exceptional skills in one particular domain, like instantly calculating large numbers, producing complex music compositions, or recalling minute details. These abilities often contrast with limitations in other areas.

- **Disability Potential**: Savant Syndrome may co-occur with other neurodevelopmental conditions, such as autism, impacting daily functioning, social interactions, or adaptability in certain environments.

- **Opportunity Potential**: Savants often excel in specialized fields related to their talents, such as mathematics, art, music, or data analysis. Their unique abilities can lead to careers in these areas or public recognition of their skills.

- **Examples**: An individual who can play a song on the piano after hearing it once, or someone who has a photographic memory and excels in recalling facts or numbers.

35. Hemispatial Neglect (Spatial Neglect)

- **Awareness**: Hemispatial Neglect, or Spatial Neglect, is a neurological condition usually caused by brain injury, where individuals fail to recognize or attend to one side of their body or visual field. It's often associated with strokes or traumatic brain injuries.

- **Manifestation**: May include failing to eat food on one side of the plate, bumping into objects on one side, or ignoring parts of the body during grooming. Individuals may be unaware of or unresponsive to stimuli on the affected side.

- **Disability Potential**: Spatial neglect can significantly impact daily functioning, including mobility, safety, and self-care tasks. Individuals may require rehabilitation and adaptation strategies to manage their environment effectively.

- **Opportunity Potential**: Those with spatial neglect often develop strong compensatory strategies and may excel in tasks that involve focused attention on a specific area or field. They often bring unique insights into neurorehabilitation and adaptive practices.

- **Examples**: Someone who needs assistance with navigating physical spaces but develops unique approaches to daily tasks, or an individual who becomes an advocate for brain injury awareness and rehabilitation.

36. Synaptic Pruning Irregularities

- **Awareness**: Synaptic Pruning Irregularities refer to differences in the brain's natural process of eliminating redundant or unused neurons during development. This process is crucial for refining neural connections. Irregularities are thought to play a role in conditions like autism and schizophrenia.

- **Manifestation**: May not be immediately visible but can affect cognitive development, sensory processing, and social behavior. Individuals may experience heightened sensitivity to stimuli or have unique patterns of neural connectivity, which can influence their learning and perception.

- **Disability Potential**: These irregularities may impact cognitive processing, sensory perception, or social functioning, depending on the condition associated with them. They can contribute to challenges in adapting to typical environments or learning at standard paces.

- **Opportunity Potential**: People with differences in synaptic pruning often have heightened pattern recognition, attention to detail, and unique cognitive pathways. They may excel in fields that benefit from atypical perspectives, such as research, technology, or the arts.

- **Examples**: An individual who notices patterns others miss or someone who excels in creative problem-solving due to different neural connections.

37. Cognitive Rigidity

- **Awareness**: Cognitive Rigidity is

characterized by difficulty adapting to new information or changing perspectives. It's often seen in conditions like autism and OCD, where there's a strong preference for routine and difficulty with flexibility in thinking.

- **Manifestation**: May look like resistance to changes in plans, difficulty shifting from one task to another, or adherence to strict routines. Individuals with cognitive rigidity might prefer structured environments and experience anxiety when routines are disrupted.

- **Disability Potential**: Cognitive rigidity can make it challenging to cope with unexpected changes, impacting daily life, work environments, and social interactions. Individuals may experience frustration or distress when routines are altered.

- **Opportunity Potential**: Those with cognitive rigidity often excel in roles requiring attention to detail, consistency, and adherence to procedures. Many thrive in structured tasks or environments where routine is valued.

- **Examples**: A person who is meticulous in routine-driven tasks or someone who excels in jobs that benefit from precision and consistency, such as data entry, accounting, or laboratory work.

38. Sensory Modulation Disorder

- **Awareness**: Sensory Modulation Disorder is a subset of Sensory Processing Disorder where individuals struggle to regulate responses to sensory stimuli. They may experience hypersensitivity (over-responsive) or hyposensitivity (under-responsive) to sounds, textures, lights, and other stimuli.

- **Manifestation**: Hypersensitive individuals might be overwhelmed by bright lights, loud noises, or crowded spaces, while hyposensitive individuals may seek out intense sensory experiences, such as deep pressure or loud sounds. Both types may exhibit unusual responses to sensory input.

- **Disability Potential**: Difficulty regulating sensory responses can make daily tasks challenging, particularly in busy or unpredictable environments. It can impact social interactions, school or work performance, and personal comfort.

- **Opportunity Potential**: Many individuals with sensory modulation issues develop strong awareness of their surroundings and can excel in environments with controlled stimuli. They may also be perceptive and empathetic, often thriving in roles that allow for sensory control.

- **Examples**: A person who seeks out a calm, quiet workspace to perform their best, or someone who thrives in careers that allow for sensory-specific work, such as roles in nature, therapeutic settings, or small team environments.

39. Stereotypic Movement Disorder

- **Awareness**: Stereotypic Movement Disorder involves repetitive, non-functional motor behaviors, such as hand-flapping, rocking, or body swaying. These behaviors are typically soothing for the individual and can increase in frequency under stress.

- **Manifestation**: Individuals may engage in repetitive physical movements, especially in situations that are anxiety-provoking or overstimulating. These behaviors may be more common in early childhood but can persist into adulthood.

- **Disability Potential**: Repetitive movements may impact social interactions, as they are sometimes misunderstood by others. In some cases, the behaviors may lead to self-injury or require management strategies in certain environments.

- **Opportunity Potential**: Individuals with

stereotypic movements often develop resilience and self-awareness as they manage these behaviors. Many excel in fields where self-regulation skills, patience, or creative expression are valued.

- **Examples**: Someone who finds creative outlets, like art or music, to channel their energy, or an individual who works well in settings where they can take sensory breaks as needed.

40. Functional Neurological Disorder (FND)

- **Awareness**: Functional Neurological Disorder is a condition where individuals experience neurological symptoms (such as tremors, seizures, or paralysis) without an identifiable structural cause. The symptoms are real and can significantly impact daily life.

- **Manifestation**: Symptoms may include non-epileptic seizures, muscle weakness, tremors, or coordination problems. These symptoms can vary widely in intensity and frequency and are often influenced by stress or emotional factors.

- **Disability Potential**: FND can limit mobility, independence, and participation in daily activities. It can impact work and social relationships, particularly when symptoms are severe or unpredictable.

- **Opportunity Potential**: Many individuals with FND develop strong self-advocacy skills and emotional resilience. They often excel in roles that allow for flexible schedules, self-management, or remote work.

- **Examples**: A person who uses their experience to advocate for awareness of invisible disabilities, or someone who thrives in a career that accommodates their unique needs, such as a remote or flexible work arrangement.

41. Cluttering

- **Awareness**: Cluttering is a speech disorder where speech is fast, irregular, or disorganized, often making it difficult for others to understand. It differs from stuttering in that it affects fluency and speech structure, rather than repeating sounds or words.

- **Manifestation**: Individuals may speak rapidly, with irregular pauses, unfinished sentences, or frequent changes in topic. Speech may sound jumbled or unclear, making communication challenging.

- **Disability Potential**: Cluttering can impact verbal communication, leading to misunderstandings and challenges in social or professional settings.

- **Opportunity Potential**: Many people with cluttering excel in creative fields where verbal expression isn't the primary focus. They may have strong written communication skills or excel in roles that value innovation.

42. Selective Mutism

- **Awareness**: Selective Mutism is an anxiety-based condition where individuals are unable to speak in specific social situations despite having the ability to speak in others. It's common in childhood but can persist into adulthood.

- **Manifestation**: May include complete silence or limited speech in certain settings, such as school or work, while being talkative in comfortable environments, like home. This silence is involuntary and often linked to social anxiety.

- **Disability Potential**: Selective Mutism can significantly impact social relationships, educational progress, and work opportunities.

- **Opportunity Potential**: Individuals with Selective Mutism may excel in written communication or find ways to express themselves through art, music, or other nonverbal means.

43. Hyperacusis

- **Awareness**: Hyperacusis is characterized by an increased sensitivity to certain frequencies and volumes of sound, often resulting in physical discomfort or pain. Common in individuals with autism and other sensory processing differences.

- **Manifestation**: Loud sounds may cause discomfort, pain, or even panic. This may lead to avoidance of noisy environments, such as concerts, busy streets, or crowded events.

- **Disability Potential**: Hyperacusis can make it difficult to participate in everyday activities that involve exposure to loud sounds, impacting both social and work environments.

- **Opportunity Potential**: Individuals with hyperacusis often develop heightened awareness and sensitivity, making them attuned to subtle auditory details. Many excel in environments that are quiet or controlled, such as research, writing, or remote work.

44. Scotopic Sensitivity Syndrome (Irlen Syndrome)

- **Awareness**: Irlen Syndrome affects how the brain processes visual information, particularly under certain lighting conditions, leading to discomfort while reading or viewing text. It's associated with light sensitivity and visual stress.

- **Manifestation**: May include headaches, eye strain, difficulty with reading comprehension, or sensitivity to fluorescent lighting. Many people find relief through colored lenses or overlays.

- **Disability Potential**: Irlen Syndrome can impact reading, academic performance, and work tasks that involve visual processing, especially under artificial lighting.

- **Opportunity Potential**: Individuals with this condition often develop strategies for managing light sensitivity and may excel in roles that allow for visual breaks or use of assistive devices.

45. Time Blindness

- **Awareness**: Time Blindness refers to difficulty perceiving the passage of time, making it hard to estimate how long tasks will take or to manage time effectively. It's common in individuals with ADHD but can also appear independently.

- **Manifestation**: Individuals may frequently lose track of time, struggle with punctuality, or find it difficult to prioritize tasks. They may rely heavily on external reminders or alarms to stay on schedule.

- **Disability Potential**: Time blindness can interfere with task management, meeting deadlines, and overall productivity in structured environments.

- **Opportunity Potential**: Many people with time blindness excel in creative fields, where they can immerse themselves deeply in tasks, or in roles that prioritize outcomes over strict schedules.

Wrap-Up: Embracing the Full Spectrum of Neurodiversity

Here we are, at the end of a chapter packed with the diverse and fascinating ways that people experience the world. Each type of neurodivergence we've explored offers a unique view into how incredible and varied the human mind can be. Some of these are well-known, like autism and ADHD, while others may have surprised you, like hyperphantasia or visual snow. But that's the beauty of neurodiversity—it's a constantly expanding spectrum, where there's always something new to understand.

Here's the thing: these aren't just labels or categories to slap on yourself or others. It's not a checklist or a set of boxes to tick off. This chapter is a snapshot of all the ways people might think, feel, and navigate the world differently. So, take it as an invitation to learn, reflect, and, most importantly, to accept yourself and others without constantly reaching for a label. If you found something here that resonated, great. Explore it, learn about it, and, if needed, talk to someone who can help you dig deeper.

The goal here isn't to box anyone in or let you off the hook for the hard work of understanding who you are. It's about making sure you know that every type of brain—whether it falls neatly into one of these categories or not—has potential and purpose. There are strengths here that might surprise you if you lean in and start to see the gifts hidden within each challenge.

So, here's your takeaway: embrace the diversity of your mind, and remember that these differences are something to be proud of. Whether you're neurodivergent, neurotypical, or somewhere in between, your unique way of thinking is valid. And if you're reading this and realize you don't fit any of these descriptions exactly, that's okay. You still bring something essential to the table.

The world is built on a foundation of diverse minds that push boundaries, drive innovation, and bring creativity to the forefront. We need each and every type of mind in this mix to keep moving forward. And no matter where you land on the spectrum, you belong here—exactly as you are.

Let's keep building a world where neurodiversity isn't just accepted but celebrated. And if you're up for it, go out there and make your own mark, embracing every part of who you are. Because that, my friend, is where your power truly lies.

SELF EMPOWERMENT
Chapter 7

Building Inner Strength and Resilience

Alright, let's get down to it: life in a neurotypical world can be rough, and it's not always going to be welcoming. You're going to come up against situations that test you, frustrate you, and sometimes make you question whether you're even on the right path. But that's exactly why you need to develop a foundation that's unshakeable—a core set of strengths, skills, and a resilient mindset that will carry you through any challenge. This section is about building a rock-solid sense of self so that, no matter what the world throws at you, you know exactly what you bring to the table and how to adapt without losing your core identity.

Embracing Your Core Strengths

Start by figuring out what you're great at—not just the skills people have complimented you on, but the things that come naturally to you. When you identify these strengths, they become tools in your toolkit, ready to deploy in any situation. You're not just surviving; you're strategizing.

- **Action Item**: Take 10-15 minutes to list out every single skill or strength you can think of, whether it's tangible or intangible. This is about getting specific. Don't just write "problem-solving." Break it down: "I'm great at identifying patterns others miss," or "I can analyze complex situations quickly." List anything from creativity and hyper-focus to analytical thinking or empathy.

- **Example**: Say you're naturally good at breaking down complex information. In a work environment, this strength could make you invaluable in team meetings, where people are struggling to see the big picture. Use it as a way to add value, to become known as the person who can turn chaos into clarity.

- **Reflection**: Once you've listed your

strengths, pick three that you rely on most often. Write down specific ways you've used these in the past to overcome challenges. This is about recognizing that you already have what it takes to handle difficult situations.

Cultivating a Growth Mindset

A growth mindset is more than just optimism; it's a decision to look at every experience as a stepping stone, not a stumbling block. You've got to become the kind of person who sees challenges and thinks, "Alright, what can I learn here?" instead of getting stuck in frustration. Growth is a choice, and it's one that puts you in the driver's seat of your own life.

Action Item: The next time you hit a setback—whether it's a project that didn't go as planned, an awkward social interaction, or a mistake at work—pause and ask yourself three questions:

What went wrong? (Be honest with yourself, but don't get caught in a blame game.)

What can I learn from this? (Identify one specific takeaway that you can apply to future situations.)

What will I do differently next time? (Turn the lesson into a concrete action step.)

Example: Let's say you struggle with keeping organized and it caused you to miss a deadline. Instead of labeling yourself as "disorganized," take a growth approach. Maybe the takeaway is that your current system doesn't work for you. Could you try a digital calendar or set up daily reminders? Use the experience as an opportunity to find solutions that align with how you operate.

Reflection: As you go through each week, make a habit of reflecting on one moment where you chose to learn instead of dwell. Document it and keep a record. This builds your mental archive of resilience. The more you practice it, the faster you'll see growth.

Personal Accountability

Now, here's where the rubber meets the road: personal accountability. This is about owning your role in every situation you're in, even if the odds aren't fair. It's easy to get caught up in frustration over things you can't control. But here's the truth: focusing on what you *can't* control leaves you powerless. Accountability puts the power back in your hands. It's the difference between saying, "This situation is hard, so I'm stuck," and saying, "This situation is hard, so what can I do about it?"

Action Item: Each morning, write down three things you'll take responsibility for that day. These don't have to be big things—they can be as simple as committing to getting through a challenging task at work or taking a moment to ground yourself during a stressful interaction.

Example: Let's say you're facing a difficult work environment where you don't feel fully understood. Rather than waiting for others to change, take responsibility for the one thing you can control: how you show up. Decide that, today, you're going to ask one clarifying question in a meeting or share one idea you've been holding back on. Taking small actions builds momentum and confidence.

Reflection: At the end of each week, review how well you followed through on your intentions. Accountability isn't about perfection; it's about progress. You're learning how to respond to your environment, and with each step, you're taking ownership of your life in ways that will compound over time.

Maximizing Your Resilience Potential

Building resilience isn't a one-time project—it's a continuous process. Every time you choose to stand back up, you're training your mind and body to handle more. You're creating a personal record of victories, no matter how small, that remind you what you're capable of. This is the kind of toughness that will carry you through, no matter what the world throws at you.

Action Item: Create a "Resilience Log." Every time you handle a situation that's hard, write it down.

Include what the situation was, how you handled it, and what you learned. This isn't just an exercise in remembering the good stuff—it's a tool for building an undeniable track record of your ability to navigate anything.

Example: Let's say you had a day where you dealt with a sensory overload situation but still managed to get through a work presentation. Write it down. Describe how you felt, what strategies you used to cope, and how you pulled yourself together for the presentation. Later, you can look back and see that, even on days that feel overwhelming, you have what it takes to succeed.

Reflection: Regularly revisit your Resilience Log to remind yourself of your capacity to handle tough moments. This will build your confidence in your own resilience, giving you the strength to face new challenges with a mindset of "I've handled tough stuff before, and I can handle it again."

Building inner strength and resilience is about mastering the art of responding instead of reacting. It's about turning every experience into an opportunity to grow, to own your life, and to thrive in ways that no one else can define for you. When you know your core strengths, adopt a growth mindset, hold yourself accountable, and actively build your resilience, you become unstoppable. No NT environment, no tough situation, and no external judgment can shake a foundation like that. You're here to play by your own rules, and the more you build on these principles, the more equipped you'll be to not just survive, but to thrive.

Practicing Self-Care for the Long Haul

Let's get one thing straight: "self-care" isn't about pampering yourself when things get tough. It's about developing habits and routines that sustain you and allow you to keep showing up. This means building a daily routine that gives you space to breathe, room to stim, and moments to ground yourself so you don't burn out. Your resilience starts with taking care of what you need in a way that's sustainable over time.

Sensory Breaks: Don't wait until you're completely overwhelmed to take a break. Schedule sensory breaks like you would any other priority. These quick resets could be as simple as stepping outside, closing your eyes, or popping in some noise-canceling headphones. They aren't optional—they're essential.

Action: When the environment gets too loud or the lights too harsh, step away for a few minutes. Find a quiet spot, stretch, take a few deep breaths, or listen to calming music. Sensory breaks keep you from reaching the point of burnout, helping you reset before things get unmanageable.

Private Stimming and Grounding Techniques: If stimming helps you manage stress or stay focused, integrate it into your routine in ways that feel comfortable. Stimming isn't something to hide; it's something to harness. Find what works for you—whether it's fidgeting, tapping, or something else—and let it be part of your daily rhythm.

Action: Keep a fidget tool or stress ball at your desk or in your bag. When you're feeling stressed or overstimulated, take a few minutes to stim and recenter. You're not indulging yourself; you're doing what you need to function at your best.

Mindfulness and Breathing: You don't need to meditate for hours to reap the benefits of mindfulness. Even a minute or two of focused breathing can ground you and reduce anxiety. This is about bringing yourself back to the present moment, especially when the demands of an NT environment start to wear you down.

Action: Set a timer on your phone for a one-minute breathing exercise a few times a day. During that minute, close your eyes, breathe deeply, and focus on the sensation of the breath. This small practice will keep you centered and give you the mental reset you need to keep going.

Setting Personal Milestones and Celebrating Small Wins

The NT world has a rigid definition of success: status, money, and climbing the corporate ladder. Forget that. Your success is about what works for you and makes you feel accomplished. Setting personal milestones that align with your own goals keeps you grounded and motivated, and celebrating small wins reinforces your progress. You're not here to chase someone else's version of success; you're here to live a life that feels right to you.

Define Success on Your Own Terms: What does success mean to you? Is it maintaining a work-life balance? Finding a job that respects your need for quiet time? These are the goals you should be aiming for. Create your own markers of achievement and stop measuring yourself against NT metrics that don't matter to you.

Action: Write down what success looks like for you. Is it completing a task without getting overwhelmed? Advocating for yourself in a tough situation? Define it, own it, and let that be your motivation. Every time you meet one of these markers, it's a win that matters.

Break Down Big Goals into Manageable Milestones: Long-term goals are overwhelming on their own, so break them down into steps you can tackle one at a time. When you take things step-by-step, you're not just making progress—you're also giving yourself the chance to celebrate along the way.

Action: Let's say you want to improve your public speaking skills. Start with speaking up once in a small meeting, then work up to presenting an idea in front of a group. Every step forward is a milestone you're hitting, so acknowledge it and let it build your confidence.

Celebrate Small Wins: It's not just about big achievements. Acknowledge every small victory along the way. You don't need anyone else's validation—take a moment to recognize and celebrate yourself.

Action: At the end of each day, jot down one thing you did well. Maybe you advocated for yourself, stuck to your routine, or avoided burnout. These small wins are proof that you're building resilience every single day.

Finding Allies and Safe Spaces

You can't spend every moment adapting. You need places and people where you can let your guard down, where you don't have to worry about masking or fitting in. These are your allies and your safe spaces—places you go to recharge, people you turn to for support. Find them, build them, and make them a regular part of your life.

Identify Allies in Your Environment: Allies are the people who understand, respect, and support you. They don't have to "get" everything about you; they just need to respect you as you are. Look for coworkers, mentors, or friends who create space for you to be authentic, and make them part of your support system.

Action: Pay attention to people who respect boundaries and seem open-minded. Strike up a conversation, ask a question, or mention a small personal need. You'll quickly see if they're willing to be supportive. Allies aren't always obvious, but once you find them, they make life in NT spaces easier.

Build a Community with Like-Minded Individuals: Find spaces where you can connect with other neurodivergent people who understand what you're going through. Whether it's an online forum, a local group, or a social media community, these connections remind you that you're not alone.

Action: Join a neurodivergent support group or an online community where people share their experiences, strategies, and encouragement. When you connect with others who get it, you're reinforcing your own resilience and building a network that keeps you grounded.

Create Personal Safe Spaces: Not all safe spaces involve other people. Sometimes, it's about having a corner of your world that's just for you—a place where you can unwind, stim freely, or just be. Set up a personal safe space that's all about recharging and letting go.

Action: Designate a spot in your home or workspace that's purely for comfort. Fill it with things that calm you, like a favorite blanket, a pair of headphones, or sensory tools. This is your space to be fully yourself without judgment, so use it whenever you need a break from NT expectations.

Creating Personal Success Metrics

Once you let go of the NT world's expectations, you have the freedom to define success on your own terms. Success doesn't have to be about status, money, or approval; it can be about growth, self-expression, and balance. Maybe it's about building a life that supports your well-being, where your work aligns with your passions, and where your relationships honor who you truly are. This isn't about lowering standards—it's about setting standards that reflect your values, your goals, and your strengths.

Defining your own success metrics means asking yourself what actually matters to you. Maybe success is mastering a skill that's challenging but rewarding. Maybe it's creating a daily routine that supports your mental health. Or maybe it's using your unique perspective to help others in ways that feel meaningful. Whatever it is, it should resonate with your core values and give you a sense of fulfillment that goes beyond any external validation.

This approach isn't about settling. It's about recognizing that true success is personal. It's about setting goals that align with your needs and strengths, and committing to them fully. When you define success on your terms, you're making the choice to live authentically, and you're giving yourself permission to pursue a path that honors who you are.

Celebrating Your Neurodivergent Identity

Living authentically as a neurodivergent individual in an NT world is, in itself, an act of success. Embracing the parts of yourself that don't conform to NT expectations is a statement of self-respect. It says that you're not willing to sacrifice your identity to fit into a mold that wasn't built with you in mind. You're here to live life on your terms, not to mute your uniqueness just to make others comfortable.

Celebrating your neurodivergent identity means recognizing the ways your mind works as strengths—not as things to fix or hide. It means viewing your differences as assets that shape your perspective, drive your creativity, and inform the way you interact with the world. Success isn't about erasing those traits; it's about letting them shine and finding ways to align them with a life that's fulfilling and empowering.

Living authentically doesn't mean ignoring the need to adapt. It means finding a balance between blending in when you need to and standing out when it counts. It's about knowing when to play by NT rules and when to rewrite them. And it's about taking pride in your neurodivergent traits, not as obstacles but as integral parts of who you are. Embracing this identity is the ultimate form of success because it allows you to live in a way that's aligned with your values and strengths—on a path that's yours, and yours alone.

YOU ARE CAPABLE OF ANYTHING
Chapter 8

After 14 years in my corporate career, I took a leap in 2014 and launched my own business—a laboratory focused on manufacturing personal care products. I was still traveling 80% of the year, but this venture was all mine, and I poured everything into it. My 11 years with a large home service company had laid a solid foundation, and I'd been part of an incredible team. We weren't just sitting in meetings; we were rolling up our sleeves and diving into the science behind new service ventures. We'd develop ideas, train technicians, and travel to put our methods into action. I learned it all—from the science of emulsions to psychrometry--the science of moisture and applied structural drying. I was like a sponge, absorbing information and applying it. I learned how to teach, how to execute, and most importantly, how to learn anything.

That's when I knew I could do just about anything I set my mind to—and that my odd, intense ideas could actually be realized. In late 2014 I took the leap, quit my career and poured everything I had into my new business.

I was **very** early to the hemp industry. I tracked down a farmer in Kentucky, one of the first involved in a pilot project to grow hemp since the ban back in the 1900s. But no one believed in the potential. Everyone told me I was insane, that I was wasting my time. I had a small side-hustle business at the back of a vape shop with a partner at the time, but even that shop owner refused to let me do business with hemp. He wouldn't even let my products in the building. And my business partner? He wanted nothing to do with hemp either. So I did what I had to—I sold my half of that business, took every cent I had, and invested it all in this new venture.

We realized that my farmer could extract the raw materials, and I could formulate products that could help people with a range of issues. Three years later, my lab had produced millions of dollars worth of products for the cannabis industry. We were doing well—not just well, but **really well**. Alongside cannabis, we branched out into food, beverage, and personal care products, but cannabis was where the big money was.

Then one night, I hit a major turning point. My love for emulsion science had led me to develop a unique process to stabilize oil-in-water emulsions for extended periods, but they would eventually separate. It was a problem that had been gnawing at me, driving me to near obsession. So, I dove headfirst into an intense, two-week hyper-focus session. I was determined to solve this. How could I get these two substances to stay blended indefinitely? I pushed myself harder than ever, digging into pharmacy science, researching, and pushing past dead ends. One night, after countless hours, I woke up with a jolt, and the answer hit me like a lightning bolt—*It's like a microwave!*

Microwaves work by vibrating water molecules until they heat up. So I thought, what if I could vibrate oil particles down to the smallest scale and encapsulate them with water? That thought led me to ultrasonic homogenizers, machines that break down oil into particles small enough to bond with water molecules, stabilized by surfactants—a concept I'd gleaned from medical journals and vaccine research. And just like that, I had developed a process for making water-soluble THC and CBD. It was revolutionary—one of the first of its kind. I proved the concept and started shopping for investors. Before long, my biggest client came forward, and we were talking acquisition. I sold the lab, and together, we launched hundreds of products—waters, sodas, drinks infused with THC and CBD. My little lab became one of the largest suppliers of bulk materials in the cannabis industry.

Then, we reached my personal goal. With the acquisition, we became the one of the first labs to supply Brazil with a prescription medication to treat epilepsy and Parkinson's. We were creating the kind of product I had once only dreamed about. And it all happened because I trusted my brain to do what it does best. I took the leap, and it paid off. But it wasn't easy. Imposter syndrome hit hard and often. Every step of the way, I questioned myself, thinking I was crazy. But each time I created a new process that worked, I found people willing to pay thousands—even millions—for my abilities.

Selling that business taught me some brutal lessons about the reality of money. I was young and naive, and I trusted people I shouldn't have. I pushed myself so hard that the stress nearly killed me. My organs started failing from the physical toll of ignoring my health. Stress will kill you, and I learned that the hard way. That experience made me who I am today. I went on to create a consultancy focused on large-scale brand IP and negotiations, applying all those lessons I learned through failure. I'd been a millionaire and lost it all, thanks to youthful stupidity and trusting the wrong people.

Trust is a major challenge for people like me. Many neurodivergent people struggle to understand the unwritten rules, and some people know exactly how to exploit that. I was naive; I just wanted to work and let the "parents" in the room take care of the things I didn't know. If I could do it over, there's a million things I'd change. But I can't. So, I'll take every lesson and keep moving forward. And hopefully, I can share these lessons with others along the way, helping them avoid some of the worst mistakes I made.

The biggest lesson learned was that I am capable of anything. So are you.

Embracing the Power of Self-Knowledge

Here we are, the final stretch. Everything you've read so far has built up to this: understanding that self-knowledge is your ultimate power source. You've peeled back layers, recognized patterns, maybe even come to terms with parts of yourself you'd overlooked or dismissed. Now it's time to use that knowledge not just to survive but to thrive. Moving forward with purpose requires that you take everything you've learned and channel it into action. This is where we get real about what it means to own your story and leverage every ounce of your neurodivergence.

Reflecting on Your Journey

Look at how far you've come. From learning about masking, decoding NT expectations, to redefining success, you've faced truths about yourself that most people spend a lifetime avoiding. Every chapter in this book has asked you to confront what it really means to navigate this world as a neurodivergent person. The point is, your journey so far has been about discovery, but moving forward means application.

When I started my own business, I didn't have all the answers. But what I did have was a relentless curiosity and a deep understanding of how my brain worked. I trusted that, despite the doubts. I learned the RISE framework through every challenge I took on, often without even knowing it. I had to **Recognize** what my unique strengths were, what my mind was capable of, and what I needed to protect myself from. I had to **Identify** the opportunities that aligned with those strengths and the potential traps along the way. I had to **Support** myself by building routines that allowed me to thrive and by cutting out distractions. And most importantly, I had to **Embrace** my journey, my setbacks, and the parts of me that didn't fit the mold.

Think about the lessons you've learned from your own experiences. Look at where you're going next, and know that every step you take forward is built on a foundation of hard-won knowledge. You've already done the hardest part—acknowledging who you are and understanding what you need.

Self-Knowledge as the Ultimate Tool

In a world that wasn't built for you, self-awareness is your biggest advantage. When you understand your own mind, you make better decisions. You see where you fit and where you don't. You navigate challenges not just with resilience but with strategy. It's not about knowing exactly what's next; it's about having the clarity to trust your own process.

This is what RISE is all about. Take it into every area of your life:

Recognize: Know your strengths. Know where you shine and where you need to be cautious. Take note of patterns, environments, and people who drain you, as well as those who lift you up.

Identify: Pinpoint opportunities where you can thrive. You don't need to be everywhere or do everything. Look for those areas where your neurodivergence gives you an edge. Lean into them.

Support: Create structures and routines that protect your energy. Set boundaries that preserve your mental health. Build a support system—find allies, mentors, and communities that understand what you're about.

Embrace: Own every part of your journey. The challenges, the breakthroughs, the moments of doubt—they're all a part of who you are. Embrace that your story is uniquely yours, and let it drive you forward.

Owning Your Story

This isn't just about introspection. Owning your story means standing up and saying, "This is who I am, and I'm not here to fit into your expectations." You've learned that neurodivergence is not something to hide or overcome; it's something to wield. It's a set of skills, insights, and perspectives that the world desperately needs but doesn't always understand. So, let them misunderstand. You're not here to make others comfortable.

Owning your story means acknowledging the parts that were hard, the mistakes you made, and the lessons you had to learn the hard way. It means recognizing that while the NT world has rules and biases, you don't have to play by them. Your story is a map of resilience and growth. It's what you've learned through trial and error. It's the path you've carved out with your own hands, and it's the blueprint for the life you're going to build.

When I look back on everything I've built, I see a story shaped by my neurodivergence, not in spite of it. I've taken risks, trusted the wrong people, and made decisions that backfired, but each one was a lesson. I can look at my journey now and see that everything I've learned along the way has led me to a place where I can live and work on my terms. That's what I want for you—to be able to look back on your story and own every chapter.

So, as you move forward, take this foundation of self-knowledge and build on it. Let it guide you, let it protect you, and most importantly, let it empower you. Embrace the parts of you that make you stand out, and let them be the reason you succeed on your own terms.

Success on Your Terms

Here's the truth: the moment you let go of NT definitions of success, you start to find freedom. Success doesn't have to mean a high-status job or social approval. It can mean cultivating a skill you're passionate about, creating a routine that supports your well-being, or making a meaningful impact on those around you. It can be as personal and unique as you are. Success is about mastery on your terms. If that means mastering a creative craft, diving into something you're passionate about, or contributing to a cause you believe in, then that's where you'll find your measure of fulfillment.

Think back to the people who doubted you along the way, the ones who said you were "wasting your time" or going off-track. Let their disbelief fuel you. Those voices will always be there, but the beauty of defining success on your terms is that their opinions don't matter. Focus on the goals that resonate with you. Don't waste time chasing someone else's version of success—it's a hollow pursuit that leads nowhere. Be bold enough to build your own vision, knowing that your neurodivergent mind is what makes that vision possible.

Staying True to Your Values

Here's the foundation: you're not just redefining success. You're aligning with your values. And when you do that, you create a life that supports your mental health, your passions, and your well-being. Think of it this way—when you live according to someone else's standards, you end up betraying yourself. But when you live by your own values, you build resilience. You know what you're about, and that self-assurance radiates into everything you do.

Living in alignment with your values isn't a side note—it's the core of real success. Sure, it might mean that you take a different path. Maybe you don't end up in the traditional nine-to-five, or you choose to pursue something that doesn't bring in a six-figure salary. But when you're true to your values, you'll find satisfaction that goes far deeper than any paycheck or title. You're building a life that strengthens your self-worth because it reflects who you really are. In a world that's constantly trying to tell you who to be, staying true to your values is a radical act of self-respect.

Embracing Flexibility and Adaptability

Let's face it—the world changes, and so do you. What worked for you five years ago might not work today, and that's normal. Neurodivergent minds often thrive in unconventional ways, and part of thriving means staying flexible. If you're willing to adapt, to pivot when something stops serving you, you're setting yourself up for lasting growth. Success isn't a straight line. It's a process of constantly evolving, of building on your strengths and adjusting to new realities.

This flexibility doesn't mean you lack direction. It means you're open to redefining your goals as you go. Don't get stuck clinging to a plan that no longer fits. Instead, focus on staying connected to your core values and let them guide you through every twist and turn. As understanding of neurodiversity continues to grow, you might find new opportunities that align better with who you've become. Let your goals grow with you. If you stay adaptable, you'll be able to handle whatever life throws your way without losing sight of what's important to you.

Success isn't about reaching a destination—it's about living in a way that reflects who you are, every single day. Redefining success on your terms means building a life that's not only sustainable but deeply fulfilling. You have the freedom to create a path that supports you, challenges you, and allows you to be exactly who you were meant to be.

You cannot do this alone. Ever. Read that again.

I know first-hand what it means to live in a neurodiverse household. Having an autistic son has opened my eyes in ways I couldn't have predicted. I've learned a lot, but there's still so much I don't fully understand. Sometimes our house is a war zone, especially now that he's in his teens. It can feel like a battle every single day, and my wife and I are in the thick of it. She's an advocate, helping parents connect with resources and find support, but we're still figuring it out ourselves. That's the reality of neurodiversity: it's an ongoing journey. You have to show up every day and work at it, staying aware of your strengths, accepting your weaknesses, and finding ways to move forward together.

If you're reading this as a parent of a neurodiverse child, I need you to hear this—you need support. Even if you feel like you've got it under control, reach out. Find every resource you can, and build a support system around your child and yourself. I think back to the early 90s when I had what would now be called an IEP (Individualized Education Plan). I didn't even realize back then that I had help behind the scenes. Without it, who knows where I'd be today? There's no shame in reaching out and asking for help—it's the opposite. It's a strength, a necessity. The path ahead is tough enough, so take whatever support you can get. Start today.

Moving Forward with Courage and Compassion

Let's be real: you're living in a world that wasn't built for you, and that takes a toll. Self-compassion isn't just a feel-good buzzword; it's the fuel that keeps you going. The NT world has rules that can feel impossible to keep up with, and setbacks are inevitable. But those setbacks don't define your worth. Self-compassion allows you to see setbacks for what they are—part of the process. They're not roadblocks, just detours, and sometimes those detours teach you more than the straight path ever could.

Self-compassion isn't about going easy on yourself or avoiding challenges. It's about recognizing that you're doing the best you can, even when things don't go according to plan. When you practice self-compassion, you build resilience because you know that each setback is a stepping stone, not a dead end. Life is going to test you, but when you're kind to yourself, you don't break. You bend, adapt, and come back stronger. Self-compassion is the foundation of resilience, and without it, every obstacle feels insurmountable. With it, those obstacles become a part of your growth.

Courage isn't the absence of fear. It's facing the uncertainty, the judgment, and the challenges and deciding to move forward anyway. If there's one thing I hope you've taken from this book, it's that neurodivergence is a strength, not a burden. You have a perspective that brings value, that disrupts the norm in the best way possible. Living with courage means showing up as yourself, every single day, even when the world doesn't always welcome that. It means trusting that who you are is enough, that your mind has something unique to offer, and that you don't have to apologize for not fitting into the NT mold.

Let the courage you build here be the fuel that propels you forward. Use it to advocate for your needs, to pursue goals that matter to you, and to create spaces where you feel authentic and empowered. Living with courage means taking the lessons you've learned, owning your story, and moving forward in a way that aligns with your values. You don't have to have it all figured out. You just have to be willing to take that next step, even if it's only a small one. Courage is the willingness to try, to fail, and to get back up with the same conviction, knowing that your journey is yours alone.

Building Empathy for Others

As you embrace your neurodivergent identity, something incredible happens. You start to understand the importance of empathy—not just for yourself but for others as well. Living openly and authentically shows the people around you that neurodiversity isn't something to hide. By embracing who you are, you're creating a ripple effect of understanding. Your openness has the power to change perceptions and make the world a more inclusive place. Empathy, in its purest form, is about recognizing that everyone is navigating their own challenges, their own neurodiversity, whether they realize it or not.

When you approach life with empathy, you're not just making room for yourself; you're making room for others, too. You're showing the world that diversity in thinking, in processing, in being, is something to celebrate. Building empathy for others starts with recognizing that while your journey is unique, you're part of a much larger community. Every time you share your story, you're helping to foster a world where neurodiversity is accepted, valued, and understood. Empathy builds bridges where walls once stood, and it's through those bridges that true change happens.

Final Thoughts

As you move forward, remember that self-compassion, courage, and empathy are more than just ideals—they're actions. They're daily choices. Choose to support yourself when things get tough. Choose to stand up for yourself and move forward with confidence. Choose to see others with understanding and to share your journey in a way that opens doors for everyone. You've come a long way, but this is just the beginning. You have the strength, the resilience, and the power to build a life that reflects who you are and to do it on your terms.

So, which is it for you? Is autism or neurodiversity something you *have*, or is it simply who you *are?*

It can be both, or one, or neither on any given day. There are moments when it feels like a disability, like a barrier that can't be ignored, and other times when it feels like an essential part of your identity, something that gives you strength and purpose. Recognize that it's never *always* one or the other. Embrace the reality that both perspectives are valid and that, sometimes, the experience of living with neurodiversity is a fluid blend of both.

Remember, not everyone will have the words to tell you their experience, and some may never be able to read these pages. But your understanding, your ability to own and articulate what this journey means to you, can be a voice for those who cannot speak it for themselves.

So, as you move forward, ask yourself: **Are you ready to live your truth, embrace the complexities, and make room for both disability and identity in your story?** Because, at the end of the day, they're both a part of what makes you exceptional.

Now it's time for you to RISE.

About The Author
Joe Bradley

Joe Bradley is an artist, entrepreneur, advocate, father, and husband--driven by a mission to reshape the way we understand and embrace neurodiversity. With over two decades of experience across corporate leadership, startups, and innovation, Joe's journey reflects resilience, curiosity, and a commitment to breaking down barriers for neurodivergent individuals.

Diagnosed with autism as an adult and a parent to an autistic son, Joe brings both personal insight and practical experience to his advocacy. His work is dedicated to empowering others to recognize the strength in neurodivergent traits and to live authentically in a world that often misunderstands them. Through his writing, consulting, and hands-on work, Joe is on a mission to inspire others to not only accept their neurodivergence but to harness it as a tool for meaningful change.

www.ingramcontent.com/pod-product-compliance
Lightning Source LLC
Chambersburg PA
CBHW020531030426
42337CB00013B/796